First World War
and Army of Occupation
War Diary
France, Belgium and Germany

2 DIVISION
99 Infantry Brigade
Machine Gun Company
26 April 1916 - 31 December 1917

WO95/1373/1

The Naval & Military Press Ltd
www.nmarchive.com
Published in association with The National Archives

Published by

The Naval & Military Press Ltd

Unit 10 Ridgewood Industrial Park,

Uckfield, East Sussex,

TN22 5QE England

Tel: +44 (0) 1825 749494

www.naval-military-press.com

www.nmarchive.com

This diary has been reprinted in facsimile from the original. Any imperfections are inevitably reproduced and the quality may fall short of modern type and cartographic standards.

© Crown Copyright

Images reproduced by permission of The National Archives, London, England, 2015.

Contents

Document type	Place/Title	Date From	Date To
Heading	WO95/1373 2 Division 99 Infy Bde 99 Machine Gun Coy		
Heading	2nd Division War Diaries 99th M.G.C. Jan-Feb. 1918		
Heading	99th MG Coy War Diary For January 1918		
War Diary	K 20 b 2.7.	01/01/1918	04/01/1918
War Diary	Rocquigny Barastre	04/01/1918	04/01/1918
War Diary	Barastre "D" Camp	04/01/1918	21/01/1918
War Diary	Barastre-Rocquigny-Metz.	22/01/1918	22/01/1918
War Diary	Metz	23/01/1918	31/01/1918
War Diary	99th MG Coy February 1918		
War Diary	Villers Pluich Sector Metz	01/02/1918	15/02/1918
War Diary	Metz	16/02/1918	28/02/1918
Heading	2nd Division 99th Brigade 99th M.G.C. From 26th April To 31st December 1916		
Heading	99th Brigade. 2nd Division. Company Disembarked Havre 26.4.16. 99th Machine Gun Company 26th-30th April 1916		
War Diary	Harve	26/04/1916	27/04/1916
War Diary	Hersin	28/04/1916	28/04/1916
War Diary	Petit Sains	29/04/1916	30/04/1916
Heading	99th Brigade/2nd Division. N 99th Machine Gun Company May 1916		
War Diary	Petit Sains	01/05/1916	03/05/1916
War Diary	Bouvigny	04/05/1916	10/05/1916
War Diary	Hersin	11/05/1916	11/05/1916
War Diary	Bruay	12/05/1916	21/05/1916
War Diary	Pt. Servins	22/05/1916	22/05/1916
War Diary	Betonval Sector	23/05/1916	31/05/1916
Heading	99th Brigade. 2nd Division. 99th Machine Gun Company June 1916		
War Diary	Bethonval Sector	01/06/1916	02/06/1916
War Diary	Camblain Labbe	03/06/1916	08/06/1916
War Diary	Carency Sector	09/06/1916	27/06/1916
War Diary	Camblain L'Abbe	28/06/1916	30/06/1916
Heading	99th Inf. Bde. 2nd Div. War Diary 99th Machine Gun Company July 1916		
Miscellaneous	99th Inf. Bde H.Q.	06/08/1916	06/08/1916
War Diary	Camblain L'Abbe.	01/07/1916	17/07/1916
War Diary	Hermain	18/07/1916	19/07/1916
War Diary	Deviel	20/07/1916	20/07/1916
War Diary	Morlancourt	21/07/1916	23/07/1916
War Diary	Haulte	24/07/1916	24/07/1916
War Diary	Montabaun	25/07/1916	25/07/1916
War Diary	Delville Wood	26/07/1916	27/07/1916
War Diary	Corbay	28/07/1916	28/07/1916
War Diary		27/07/1916	31/07/1916
War Diary	Bromfay Farm	31/07/1916	31/07/1916
Heading	99th Brigade. 2nd Division. 99th Brigade Machine Gun Company August 1916		

Heading	War Diary of 99th Machine Gun Company From Aug 1st- Aug 31st 1916		
War Diary	In The Field	01/08/1916	31/08/1916
Heading	99th Brigade. 2nd Division 99th Machine Gun Company September 1916		
Miscellaneous	D.A.G. 3rd Echelon. Herewith copy of War Diary for September		
War Diary	Hebuterne Sector	01/09/1916	20/09/1916
War Diary	Bois Du Warnimont	21/09/1916	25/09/1916
War Diary	Ref Hebuterne 1/10,000	26/09/1916	29/09/1916
War Diary	Courcelles-au-Bois	30/09/1916	30/09/1916
Heading	99th Brigade. 2nd Division. 99th Machine Gun Company October 1916		
War Diary	Courcelles	01/10/1916	02/10/1916
War Diary	Mailly	03/10/1916	07/10/1916
War Diary	Raincheval	08/10/1916	16/10/1916
War Diary	Mailly	16/10/1916	21/10/1916
War Diary	Bertrancourt	22/10/1916	29/10/1916
War Diary	Mailly	30/10/1916	31/10/1916
Heading	99th Brigade. 2nd Division. 99th Machine Gun Company November 1916		
Heading	War Diary of November 1916		
War Diary	Mailly-Maillette	01/11/1916	06/11/1916
War Diary	Mailly	07/11/1916	13/11/1916
War Diary	View Trench	13/11/1916	17/11/1916
War Diary	Sarton	17/11/1916	17/11/1916
War Diary	Terra-Mesnil	18/11/1916	18/11/1916
War Diary	Beauval	19/11/1916	20/11/1916
War Diary	Berneuil	21/11/1916	22/11/1916
War Diary	Mesnil Domqueur	23/11/1916	23/11/1916
War Diary	Argenvillers	24/11/1916	24/11/1916
War Diary	Drucat	25/11/1916	26/11/1916
War Diary	Hanchy	27/11/1916	30/11/1916
Heading	99th Brigade. 2nd Division. 99th Machine Gun Company December 1916		
War Diary	Hanchy	01/12/1916	31/12/1916
Heading	2nd Division 99th Infy Bde 99th Machine Gun Coy. Jan-Dec 1917		
Heading	99th Brigade/2nd Division. 99th Machine Gun Company : : : January 1917		
War Diary	Hanchy	01/01/1917	08/01/1917
War Diary	Domesmont	09/01/1917	10/01/1917
War Diary	Terra-Mesnil	11/01/1917	12/01/1917
War Diary	Buzincourt	13/01/1917	19/01/1917
War Diary	Aveluy	20/01/1917	27/01/1917
War Diary	R 29 Central	28/01/1917	31/01/1917
Heading	99th Brigade/2nd Division. 99th Machine Gun Company : : : February 1917		
Heading	99th Machine Gun Coy Vol XI		
War Diary		01/02/1917	04/02/1917
War Diary	Bouzincourt	05/02/1917	23/02/1917
War Diary	Usna Hill	24/02/1917	28/02/1917
Heading	99th Brigade/2nd Division. 99th Machine Gun Company : : : March 1917		
Heading	99th M.G. Co March 1917 Vol 12		
War Diary	Usna Hill	01/03/1917	03/03/1917

Type	Description	From	To
War Diary	670 SE 1/20000 R 29 Central	03/03/1917	10/03/1917
War Diary	Below Trench	10/03/1917	10/03/1917
War Diary	Albert	11/03/1917	14/03/1917
War Diary	Usna Hill	15/03/1917	18/03/1917
War Diary	Albert	19/03/1917	24/03/1917
War Diary	Contay	25/03/1917	25/03/1917
War Diary	Ampliers	26/03/1917	26/03/1917
War Diary	Bonnieres	27/03/1917	27/03/1917
War Diary	Blangersmont	28/03/1917	31/03/1917
Heading	99th Brigade/2nd Division. 99th Machine Gun Company : : : : April 1917		
Miscellaneous	99th MG Coy War Diary For April 1917		
War Diary	Sains Les Pernes	01/04/1917	09/04/1917
War Diary	A 24 C 60	10/04/1917	20/04/1917
War Diary	51B N.W.A 2867.9	21/04/1917	01/05/1917
Heading	99th Brigade/2nd Division. 99th Brigade Machine Gun Company : : : May 1917		
War Diary	51B N.W.A 2867.9	01/05/1917	03/05/1917
War Diary	Lens Sheet 11	04/05/1917	16/05/1917
War Diary	Lens. 11	17/05/1917	31/05/1917
Heading	99th Brigade/2nd Division. 99th Machine Gun Company : : : June 1917		
Heading	99th M G Coy June 1917		
War Diary	Sheet. 51B N. W. B 15 Central.	01/06/1917	19/06/1917
War Diary	Bethune Combined Sheet	20/06/1917	30/06/1917
Heading	99th Brigade/2nd Division. 99th Machine Gun Company : : : July 1917		
War Diary	Annequin	01/07/1917	31/07/1917
Heading	99th Brigade/2nd Division. 99th Machine Gun Company : : : August 1917		
Heading	99th M.G. Coy August 1917 Vol 17		
War Diary	Annequin	01/08/1917	25/08/1917
War Diary	Annezin	25/08/1917	31/08/1917
Heading	99th Brigade/2nd Division. 99th Machine Gun Company : : : September 1917		
Heading	September 1917 Vol 18		
War Diary	Annezin	01/09/1917	05/09/1917
War Diary	Annezin Gorre	06/09/1917	07/09/1917
War Diary	Le Plantin	08/09/1917	18/09/1917
War Diary	Annequin	19/09/1917	30/09/1917
Heading	99th Brigade/2nd Division. 99th Machine Gun Company : : : October 1917		
Heading	99th Machine Gun Cay for October 1917. Vol 19		
War Diary	Annequin North	01/10/1917	01/10/1917
War Diary	Cambrin Sector	01/10/1917	04/10/1917
War Diary	Annequin & Oblinghem	05/10/1917	05/10/1917
War Diary	Auchel	06/10/1917	17/10/1917
War Diary	Cauchy-A-La-Tour.	18/10/1917	31/10/1917
Operation(al) Order(s)	99th Machine Gun Coy Operation Order No 80	25/10/1917	25/10/1917
Operation(al) Order(s)	99th Machine Gun Company. Operation Order No. 81	31/10/1917	31/10/1917
Heading	99th Brigade/2nd Division. 99th Machine Gun Company : : : : November 1917		
Heading	99th Machine Gun Coy. November 1917		
War Diary	Cauchy A La Tour	01/11/1917	04/11/1917
War Diary	Robeck	05/11/1917	05/11/1917
War Diary	Estaires	06/11/1917	06/11/1917

War Diary	Eecke	07/11/1917	07/11/1917
War Diary	Winnezeele	08/11/1917	23/11/1917
War Diary	Baraste	24/11/1917	24/11/1917
War Diary	Beaumetz-Les Cambrai	25/11/1917	30/11/1917
Heading	99th Brigade/2nd Division. 99th Machine Gun Company : : : December 1917		
Heading	99th M.G. Coy December 1917 Vol 21		
War Diary	Map Ref E 27	01/12/1917	04/12/1917
War Diary	K 20 b	04/12/1917	31/12/1917

WO 95/1373
2 Divisional
20 Infty Bde
99 machine gun Coy

2nd Division
War Diaries
99th M.G.C.
JAN - FEB.
1918

Box 1373

Army Form C. 2118.

WAR DIARY
or
INTELLIGENCE SUMMARY.
(Erase heading not required.)

99 L.G. Coy
War Diary for
January
1918

Vol 22

WAR DIARY
INTELLIGENCE SUMMARY

Army Form C. 2118.

OC "A" Machine Gun Coy

Place	Date	Hour	Summary of Events and Information	Remarks and references to Appendices
K20.b.2.7	Jan 1 to Jan 14		Coy continue to hold same position on the line as in Battery part of December 1917. Coy HQ and transport lines remain at VELU WOOD. 2/Lt A.A. BUNDEY returned from leave to U.K.	Ref map MOEUVRES 1/20,000
	Jan 15		Coy relieved in the line by No 236 m.g. Coy and Lt J. Hope. Extract from O.O.99:- "The Coy will be relieved in the line on the night 14th/15th January by the 236th m.g. Coy and North I Hope. The 2 guns on JUHA Sap and K 25.9.18. will be relieved by the N. I. Hope. 2 guns on K26a will be relieved by the 236 m.g. Coy. "C" Battery will not be relieved, but will evacuate their position as soon as light permits and Limbers arrive. On relief teams and Limbers will proceed to the SAG HEAP 13x C.8.2 to await arrival of HQrs and thereafter proceed to BARASTRE.	
ROCQUIGNY- BARASTRE			On relief Gun teams entrained on Light Railway at J31d (moeuvres) and detrained at ROCQUIGNY railhead, marching thence to (30,000) "D" Camp BARASTRE. Limbers proceeded by road to BARASTRE, transport lines.	

Army Form C. 2118.

WAR DIARY
or
INTELLIGENCE SUMMARY.
(Erase heading not required.)

Place	Date	Hour	Summary of Events and Information	Remarks and references to Appendices
BARASTRE "D" Camp	Jan 4th		Transport Lines moved from VELU WOOD to BARASTRE "D" CAMP. CAPT. A.P. SKEVINGTON, LIEUT R.L. WALL awarded M.C. for Operations at Nov 30 1917. 8 ORs awarded military medal, 1 CR awarded bar to M.M. for same operation.	A.P. Skevington Lt Col
"	5th		2/Lt R.J. GRIFFITH proceeded on trial to French South Army M.G. School at CHALONS-SUR-MARNE. Lieut B.J. Drake joined Bn on appointment from M.G. Base Depot.	
"	6th Sunday		Quiet Day. Corpl Beadel proceeded to M.G. Base G.H.Q. S.A. Sch. 2/Lt G.E. Backhouse proceeded on leave.	
"	7th		2/Lt of foot baths. Romanov carried out repairs and work in the Camp. 2/Lt W. Ackland returned from Leave.	
"	8th		CAPT. A.P. SKEVINGTON, M.C., attended Divisional Conference held at ROCQUIGNY at 2.15 pm. Coy baths at the Baths, BARASTRE during morning from 9am to 12.30 pm. Kit Inspection in Afternoon.	

Army Form C. 2118.

WAR DIARY
or
INTELLIGENCE SUMMARY.
(Erase heading not required.)

Place	Date	Hour	Summary of Events and Information	Remarks and references to Appendices
BARARA "D" Camp	Jan 8th		Repairs continued and finished also for protection against stake aircraft. Shelter trenches dug for drawing the camp.	
	9th		Stores built under the supervision of R.E.'s. Parade in huts. Lt. Col STRETTELL-MILLER died on attachment from H.Q. Base Depot.	Wilson H. Gordon Commanding 3rd Inf. Coy.
	10th		Parade in huts. Overhauling of our equipments	
	11th		Revd V. St CLARE Hill assumed temporary command afts by 1st sec Cpt A.P. SKEVINGTON. Proceeded on leave to UK. Bts Armoured & mobile Guns and Gun Equipment working parties in the Camp. Guns fired on the range.	
	12th		No 1 and 2 Sections under Section Officers on Camp fatigue. No 3 and 4 Sections employed on Camp fatigue.	
	13th (Sun)		Quiet day. Football match v/ 99th Inf. in afternoon.	
	14th		Lieut. Colonel Brook, A.S.C. inspected the Transport Lines. Got rifles during the morning. Major General Conrad 2nd Division inspected Camp in afternoon.	

WAR DIARY
INTELLIGENCE SUMMARY
(Erase heading not required.)

Army Form C. 2118.

Place	Date	Hour	Summary of Events and Information	Remarks and references to Appendices
BARASTRE and D. Camp	Jan 15		Parade in Camp. Gen. Bn. Bomb Drill etc. No 2 Section employed on Camp Fatigues	Arthur Luckhew Commdg. Officer
	16		Coy employed on Parade and Fatigues in the Camp. 2) Attd 16a and 101 attended a demonstration in use of mortars at Ytres	
	17		Coy engaged cleaning up Camp etc. Coy attended Illumination demonstration at 0100655 at 10.30pm. No 1 Section engaged on Camp Fatigue. No 2 Section engaged on Camp Fatigue. Barrage Drill etc.	
	18		Parade in Camp	
	19			
	20 (Sun)		Coy games through Gas Chamber in morning Football match 6th M.G.C. in afternoon. Lead V. 5th - lost 1Pt. Reconnoitre line in VILLERS-PLOUICH Sector.	
	21		Coy paraded under Section Officer for overhauling of kit, equipment and fighting Limbers. W.O. Reardon and NCOs attended demonstration in use of Canne Signal.	

Coy bathed

Army Form C. 2118.

WAR DIARY
or
INTELLIGENCE SUMMARY.
(Erase heading not required.)

Place	Date	Hour	Summary of Events and Information	Remarks and references to Appendices
BARASTRE – ROCQUIGNY – METZ	22		Coy. less transport paraded at 9.20 a.m. and marched to ROCQUIGNY, where they entrained on Lgt. Railway to METZ. Transport and details proceeded the METZ by road. OC's Transport and Coy. billeted in METZ.	
METZ	23		2/Lt. A.W. Hand admitted to hospital. Burial at BARASTRE to Rm out by 223 M.G. Coy. (R.N.D.) 2/Lt G.E. BRICKHOUSE returns from leave. Lieut. I. St. Clare Shu and 2/Lt G.E. Brickhouse reconnoitred the line in "A" & "B" Sub-Sectors. 8.30 a.m. 25 O.R.'s No. 2 Section paraded under 2/Lt. Acheland for Rt. Latigue 12.30 pm 25 O.R. No. 3 Section paraded under Lieut. Arthelow – men to Rt. Tatigue. Lieut. I. St. Claredus attended Group Commanders and Sect. Sections assumed command of Coy. and relief of 188 M.G. Coy. in relieve on morning of 24th.	
	24th			

Army Form C. 2118.

WAR DIARY
or
INTELLIGENCE SUMMARY.
(Erase heading not required.)

Place	Date	Hour	Summary of Events and Information	Remarks and references to Appendices
METZ	Jan 24th		Extract from O.O. No 100. "The 99th M.G. Coy will relieve the 188th M.G. Coy in the line on morning of 24th inst.	
			1. No 1 Section two 1 team will parade at 2am under Lieut B.J. Drake and will proceed to Charing Cross. They will take over F1 position. Guides will be at Charing X at 3.45am	
			2. No 2 Section two 1 teams will parade at 2.30am under 2/Lt W. Ockland. They will take over I.1, I.2 posts.	
			3. No 1 Section and 1 team of No 3 Section will parade at 2am under 2/Lt A.A. Bundey. They will take over I.16 position.	
			4. Remaining 3 teams of No 3 Section will parade at 3.30am under Lieut Crutchlow - Willer. They will take over R.1 position	
			5. 1 Team of No 1 Section and 1 team of No 2 Section and Coy HQ's will parade at 3.30am under Lt D.A. Watson	
			Coy HQ will be in FIFTEEN RAVINE (RIGA Cenk.) LA VACQUERIE 1 to 2.3	
			Rear HQs and Transport Lines remain at METZ	
	25th		2 drivers, 2 mules and 1 man wounded by Hostile Aircraft bomb in TRESCAULT whilst taking rations to the line	
	26th		Nothing to report.	

Army Form C. 2118.

WAR DIARY
— OF —
INTELLIGENCE SUMMARY.
(Erase heading not required.)

Place	Date	Hour	Summary of Events and Information	Remarks and references to Appendices
METZ	Jan 27		Capt A.J. Sherrington M.C., O.C., returned from leave and assumed Command of Coy. Lieut. V. St. Polowska relinquished duties of Coy Commander and resumed duties of 2nd in Command. 2/Lt W. Backhouse proceeded to R.T.O. Toenor. 2/Lt Griffiths returned from road to South French Army CHALONS-SUR-MARNE. School from op. 101.	
	28		1. An instruction relative to Paris Leave was the night 28/29th inst. 2(a) 2/Lt C.W. Shelton - shelton with the teams of No.3 Section at [?] from 1am will move and be relieved by 2/Lt W. Ackland with teams of No.2 Section at 11 pm. (b) 2/Lt A.A. Bundy with teams of No4 Section at 11.6 pm will relieve and be relieved by Lieut B.J. Batt with teams of No.1 Section at F.1 pm. Notice Aircraft bombing in vicinity of METZ.	
	29.		Lieut J.J. Watson to Rear H.Q. Heavy hostile aircraft bombing in vicinity of METZ.	

Army Form C. 2118.

WAR DIARY
or
INTELLIGENCE SUMMARY.
(Erase heading not required.)

Place	Date	Hour	Summary of Events and Information	Remarks and references to Appendices
METZ	Jan 30		Extract OO 102. 1. The 3 teams of No 4 Sections at 1,2 and 6 portion and the one team of No 3 Section at 5 portion will be relieved on the night of 30th/31st inst. by "B" Section of the 283rd M.G. Coy. On relief all four teams will proceed to METZ	A.Skirl-Lngh Captain D/6
	31.		Teams of No 3 and 4 Sections relieved by 283rd M.G. Coy reported at METZ.	

Army Form C. 2118.

WAR DIARY
—or—
INTELLIGENCE SUMMARY.
(Erase heading not required.)

WA 23

99th Inf Bde
February 1918

Army Form C. 2118.

WAR DIARY
INTELLIGENCE SUMMARY.
(Erase heading not required.)

99th M.G. Coy.
February 1918

Place	Date	Hour	Summary of Events and Information	Remarks and references to Appendices
VILLERS PLUICH SEP. 1 SECTOR to METZ Feb 5			12 Guns of the Coy remain in the line. Dispositions adal end of January. Comforts Section of 3 and 4 Sections in reserve at METZ. Rear HQrs and transport lines in METZ.	
	1st		2/Lt. R.I. Griffiths proceeds on leave to UK.	
	3rd		2/Lt A.W. Perry proceeded on leave to UK. L/Cpl Hawson E. to V Corps Gas School for course.	
	6th 2am Hand over		Coy relieved in the line by the 5th M.G. Coy. Billets furnished occupies by the 5th M.G. Coy in METZ taken over.	
	7th 8am		Coy work in METZ. 2 working parties proceed daily Consisting of 2 officers NCOs and 20 men for work at Q.28.6.9.	
	10th 5am		Adv Bde H.Q. 9.2.18 "On the night of 9th/10th inst 99th M.G. Coy. No 1 Section will relieve the 5th M.G. Coy No. 1 Section. Disposition of Guns & teams of No 1 Section under 2/Lt G.E. STOCKHOUSE will take over S.J. and S.2. 3 Teams of No 2 Section under 2/Lt ACKLAND will take over the	

WAR DIARY
INTELLIGENCE SUMMARY

Army Form C. 2118.

99th M.G. Coy
Feb 1918

Place	Date	Hour	Summary of Events and Information	Remarks and references to Appendices
VILLERS BOCAGE SECTOR METZ	10.		Op Ods No continued. 1 Team of No 1 Section & 1 team of No 2 Section under Lieut ByBake were over. The 1 Team proceeded to R.L. 1 Tripod and M.G.O gun from No 4 taken over. No 3 Section will be ready to move at 15min. The 4 will be ready to move at 30min. No 3 Section will be in Divisional Reserve at METZ. The guns, tripods, belt boxes of this section will be kept permanently packed.	
	11th		Section in Reserve took up huts and general improvements. This Section to be ready to move at one hours notice. Nothing to report.	
	12/13			
	14.		2/Lt A.A. BINDER and Sgt. HANNAN proceed to CAMIERS for Course	
	15.		No 2 Section relieved by No 3 Section under Lieut Stretton in the	

Army Form C. 2118.

WAR DIARY
or
INTELLIGENCE SUMMARY. February 1918.
(Erase heading not required.)

Place	Date	Hour	Summary of Events and Information	Remarks and references to Appendices
METZ			Lieut V. St Blanche proceeded on Leave	Wilkinson Captain Commanding
	17/1/18		Lieut J.A Watson From Command	
			Nothing to report.	
	19		No 2 Section under Lt Ackland relieves No 1 Section under Lieut B.J. Drake.	
			Lt L.J. Griffiths from Leave.	
	20		Lieut J.A Watson proceeds on Leave.	
	21		2nd Lt A.W Perry from Leave	
	22		2nd Lt Austerry relieves W. Mackland.	
	23		Lt H. Ackland to Hospl. Roads, & and Rails moved to huts on North rd of METZ-FINS ROAD.	
	24		No 1 Section under Lieut Drake relieves No 4 Section under Lt Mackrovie. Transport lines moves hade Canvas locd of NEUVILLE - EQUANCOURT ROAD	

Army Form C. 2118.

WAR DIARY
INTELLIGENCE SUMMARY.
(Erase heading not required.)

Feby 1918

Place	Date	Hour	Summary of Events and Information	Remarks and references to Appendices
METZ	25/2/18		Nothing to report.	

2nd Division
99th Brigade
99th M. G. C.
From 26th April To 31st December
1916

Box 1323

99th Brigade.
2nd Division.

Company disembarked HAVRE 26.4.16.

99th MACHINE GUN COMPANY

26th-30th APRIL 1 9 1 6

WAR DIARY
or
INTELLIGENCE SUMMARY

(Erase heading not required.) 99 Machine Gun Company

Army Form C. 2118.

Place	Date	Hour	Summary of Events and Information	Remarks and references to Appendices
Havre	26/4/16		The Company arrived in Havre Harbour from Southampton about 3.30 am on two boats. 8 Officers and 85 N.C.O's and men being on the S.S. Connaught and 2 Officers and 58 N.C.O's and men on the R.M.T. MAIDAN with the Transport. At 7.30 am the Company started to disembark this work went on till about 11 pm when the Company moved off and marched to No 5 Rest Camp where we were put under Canvas, and received orders to move next morning at 11.30 am	
Havre	27/4/16		At 10.30 am the Company paraded and marched to the GARE MARITIME where we entrained, on completion, the train moved out at 1.30 pm passing through ROUEN and DARNETAL. An uneventful journey brought us to HERSIN	
HERSIN	28/4/16		We arrived at HERSIN about 5.30 am which is the Railhead. The Company detrained and marched to SAINS EN GOHELLE where I reported to the Divisional Head Quarters. From there we were sent on to Billet-	

Army Form C. 2118.

WAR DIARY
or
INTELLIGENCE SUMMARY
(Erase heading not required.)

99 Machine Gun Company

Place	Date	Hour	Summary of Events and Information	Remarks and references to Appendices
VERSIN	28/4/16		at PETIT SAINS & FOSSE 10. The Transport were sent on to Billet at BOYEFFLES. The rest of the day was spent in settling the Company down. I reported our arrival to the Brigadier Lieut-Col Barker	
PETIT SAINS	29/4/16		The day was spent in cleaning up after the journey. I went for a tour round a part of the trenches accompanied by the B.M.G.O. Capt Grout Royal Fusiliers. At 3pm The Company was inspected by the Brigadier General Lieut Col Barker who seemed pleased with what he saw	
PETIT SAINS	30/4/16		The morning was spent in inspecting Arms and equipment and in doing drill. In the evening 4 Officers: 2/Lieuts Fletcher Barratt Bickerton, Moritz, Crawford, and 28 NCO's and men went up to the trenches for a tour of duty & instruction	

99th Brigade.
2nd Division.

N   99th MACHINE GUN COMPANY

          M A Y   1 9 1 6

Army Form C. 2118.

WAR DIARY
or
INTELLIGENCE SUMMARY

(Erase heading not required.) 96 Machine Gun Company Vol 2

Place	Date	Hour	Summary of Events and Information	Remarks and references to Appendices
PETIT SAINS	1/5/16		The morning was spent in doing Arm drill and a Route march In the Afternoon The Company did Gun drill. In the evening rations were sent to the people in the trenches belonging to the Company	
PETIT SAINS	2/5/16		The morning was spent in firing and testing new guns which we drew just before leaving England. The afternoon was spent in cleaning up guns after firing in the morning. The party in the trenches were relieved by Sgt N.C.O's & men.	
PETIT SAINS	3/5/16		The Company received orders to move to BOUVIGNY and Billet there. The transport to remain at BOYEFFLES. The move was carried out at 11-30 am. The Company arriving in their new Billet about 12.30 pm the CHATEAU at BOUVIGNY. Two men were Killed in the Trenches by shell fire:- Ptes Eden and HALLS and were Buried at AIX NOULETTE	
BOUVIGNY	4/5/16		The day was spent in cleaning up very little work could be done as men had to be kept under cover owing to the place being shelled 2/Lieut P BICKERTON commanding of the trenches + was admitted to Hospital	

Army Form 118.

WAR DIARY
or
INTELLIGENCE SUMMARY

(Erase heading not required.)

99 Company Machine Gun Corps

Instructions regarding War Diaries and Intelligence Summaries are contained in F. S. Regs., Part II. and the Staff Manual respectively. Title Pages will be prepared in manuscript.

Place	Date	Hour	Summary of Events and Information	Remarks and references to Appendices
BOUVIGNY	4/5/16		In the evening Relief took place in the trenches 2 Lieuts FERRIER, HEAL, McCULLAGH and GALLICHAN and 26 N.C.O's + men relieving those already in. 8 Guns were also sent up to relieve those already in as they belonged to other Brigades. No Casualties	
BOUVIGNY	5/5/16		A quiet day. The men in billets spent the day doing fatigues etc. No Casualties	
BOUVIGNY	6/5/16		A quiet day. The men in billets doing fatigues. a party of 25 N.C.O's and men went on fatigue to the trenches carrying Bombs. In the evening 26 N.C.O's and men relieved those already in the trenches. No Casualties	
Pt of BOUVIGNY	7/5/16		A quiet day. The men in billets doing fatigues. In the afternoon a party of 50 N.C.O's + men went on fatigue to the trenches carrying Bombs. No Casualties	
BOUVIGNY	8/5/16		A quiet day. The men in billets doing fatigues. In the evening 2 Lieuts MORITZ and CRAWFORD and 34 N.C.O's and men relieved those already in the trenches. On relief the men relieved returned to billets at BOUVIGNY. No Casualties	

Army Form C. 2110.

WAR DIARY
or
INTELLIGENCE SUMMARY

(Erase heading not required.)

99 Company Machine Gun Corps

Instructions regarding War Diaries and Intelligence Summaries are contained in F. S. Regs., Part II. and the Staff Manual respectively. Title Pages will be prepared in manuscript.

Place	Date	Hour	Summary of Events and Information	Remarks and references to Appendices
BOUVIGNY	9/5/16		A quiet day. The men in billets doing fatigues. In the evening the men in the trenches were relieved by the 21st Brigade Machine Gun Company on completion. The men returned to their billets at Bouvigny. No Casualties.	
BOUVIGNY	10/5/16		Orders have been received that the Brigade will be relieved during the night 10/11th May, on completion the Brigade move back for rest and refitting. The Company having already been relieved paraded at 5-15pm and marched to HERSIN where we were billeted for the night, having received orders to move next day to BRUAY.	
HERSIN	11/5/16		The morning was spent in packing. At 1pm the Company paraded and moved off, marching via BARLIN to BRUAY arriving about 3-30pm where we were billeted.	
BRUAY	12/5/16		The day was spent in overhauling Guns, Ammunition and equipment. The work kept the Company employed all day.	

Army Form C. 2118.

WAR DIARY
or
INTELLIGENCE SUMMARY

(Erase heading not required.) 99. Company. Machine Gun Corps.

Place	Date	Hour	Summary of Events and Information	Remarks and references to Appendices
Annay	12/5/16		The undermentioned N.C.O's + Men were attached to the Company.	
			22. R.F.	
			1 Sgt. 3 L/Cpls. 25. Privates. Total — 29 all ranks.	
			⊙ 23. R.F.	
			2 Sgt. 5 L/Cpls. 15 Privates. Total — 22 " "	
			✗ 1. R. Berks.	
			2 Sgt. 6 L/Cpls. 17 Privates. " — 24 " "	
			K.R.R.C.	
			1 a/Sgt. 1 Cpl. 15 Privates " — 17 " "	
			Grand Total 92 " "	
			Including :—	
			✗ a/C.S.M. 1 ⊙ a/C.Q.M.Sgr	
			They were posted as under :—	
			22. R.F. 1 N.C.O's + 22 Men to No. 1. Section.	
			1. R. Berks	
			2. N.C.O's + 22 Men to No. 2. " "	

Army Form C. 2118.

WAR DIARY
or
INTELLIGENCE SUMMARY

(Erase heading not required.)

99 Company, Machine Gun Corps.

Place	Date	Hour	Summary of Events and Information	Remarks and references to Appendices
BRUAY.	16/5/16		General. Morning was spent in Route March stopping at 8 a.m & returning at 12 noon. Afternoon; the Company bathed. In the afternoon the Company was paid out.	
BRUAY.	17/5/16		Paraded at 8 a.m & marched to BOIS LOUIS where Nos. 1 & 2 Sections conducted firing practices, testing hyposcopes etc. No 3 & 4 Sections had a Tactical Scheme. Returned at 8.45 p.m.	
BRUAY.	18/5/16		The Company was engaged in digging :- At 6.30 a.m. 75 Men under 2/Lt. S. Head & M. McCullagh were sent to R.13.B.4.4. R.1.C.1.1. " " 25 " " " 2/Lt. D. Crawford " " " " " R.19.d.5.4. " " 8.30 p.m 50 " " " A.J. French	
BRUAY	19/5/16		In the morning the Company was engaged in cleaning limbers & packing them. In the afternoon action from limbers was practised.	
BRUAY.	20/5/16		The Company was engaged in Brigade Scheme at ; Trench Warfare.	

2449 Wt. W14957/M90 750,000 1/16 J.B.C. & A. Forms/C.2118/12.

Army Form C. 2118.

WAR DIARY or INTELLIGENCE SUMMARY

(Erase heading not required.)

99th Company Machine Gun Corps

Instructions regarding War Diaries and Intelligence Summaries are contained in F. S. Regs., Part II. and the Staff Manual respectively. Title Pages will be prepared in manuscript.

Place	Date	Hour	Summary of Events and Information	Remarks and references to Appendices
BRUAY	21/5/16		The Company paraded at 9.a.m.; marched to HERSIN. 2/Lt K. FLETCHER – BARRETT was left until 1 p.m. to collect claims. There were no claims received. On the night of 21st – 22nd the Company moved from HERSIN to Pt. SERVINS. 2nd i/c was sent forward to take over billets.	
Pt. SERVINS	22/5/16		The Company paraded at 6 a.m. marched to VILLERS-au-BOIS, where it was billeted. 8 Officers 185 N.C.O.s & Men with 16 guns, ammunition etc paraded for relief to the line. Company went into action in the evening. Casualties – 2 men wounded.	
BETONVAL SECTOR VILLERS au BOIS	23/5/16		Quiet day with little shelling. Reinforcement of 20 men were sent up to the line. No Casualties.	
"	24/5/16		Men in billets spent the day in doing fatigues etc. In the evening a relief of 7 N.C.Os & 161 men took place. No Casualties. Capt C. GRANT assumed Command of the Company, vice Capt RICKETTS.	
"	25/5/16		Day in billets spent in general fatigue, cleaning kit etc. No Casualties.	
"	26/5/16			
"	27/5/16		The Company moved into billets at CAMBLAIN L'ABBÉ. No Casualties.	

Army Form C. 2118.

WAR DIARY
or
INTELLIGENCE SUMMARY

(Erase heading not required.)

99th Company Machine Gun Corps

Place	Date	Hour	Summary of Events and Information	Remarks and references to Appendices
BETONVAL SECTOR	28/9/16		Day in billets spent in cleaning billets etc. Transport moved to Pr. SERVINS. In evening relief of 4 N.C.O's & 24 Men were sent up to the line. No Casualties.	
	29/9/16		Day in billets spent in general fatigue. No Casualties.	
	30/9/16		Brigade fatigue in evening. No Casualties.	
	31/9/16		Day in billets spent in cleaning billets. No Casualties.	

99th Brigade.
2nd Division.

99th MACHINE GUN COMPANY

JUNE V 1916

99 Company Machine Gun Corps Vol 3

Place	Date	Hour	Summary of Events and Information	Remarks and references to Appendices
~~CAMBLAIN~~	1/4		Relief of 1 N.C.O. & 10 men sent up to the line. Company in action. Casualties 1 officer & 3 men wounded, 1 man killed. 3 guns out of action.	
BETHONVAL SECTOR	2/4		Relief of 1 N.C.O. & 3 men sent up to line. Reinforcement of 6 men sent up from Base. No Casualties	
CAMBLAIN L'ABBÉ	3/4		Company was relieved by 5th Inf. Bde. M.G. Company & returned to billets at CAMBLAIN L'ABBÉ. No Casualties. Morning & afternoon spent in unpacking limbers.	
"	4/4		Spent in billets CAMBLAIN L'ABBÉ.	
"	5/4		do.	
"	6/4		do. Officers had Tactical lecture from G.O.C. 99 Inf Bde.	
"	7/4		Transport Inspection by O.C. II Div Train. New bivi reconnoitered	
"	8/4		99 M.G.C. relieved 5th M.G.C. in CARENCY Sector will 11 Guns. Disposition as to coy. H.Q. of Company moved to 130 ALLEY.	Apx I
CARENCY SECTOR	9/4		Additional Gun moved up to CARENCY line.	
	10		Remaining 4 guns moved up in reserve to CARENCY sector, and Rest in reserve in 130 ALLEY.	
	14		One of Reserve Guns moved up to SERGATZ ALLEY. This was final Disposition of guns and is shown on mat.	- 2

Place	Date	Hour	Summary of Events and Information	Remarks and references to Appendices
CARENCY SECTOR	15/16/24		Trench routine: Seven covered emplacements built i.e. S1, S2, S3, S4, S5 R.5, R6. Much work done on dugouts which were greatly improved.	
CARENCY SECTOR	24		Preliminary work on "GEORGE - SAPS" being kept open S. of MONTGER E. of BRISSON, and E. of IRISH ALLEY. Night firing along the whole Bde area.	Appendix 2
CARENCY SECTOR	25	-	As for 24	
	26	-	18 M.G.C. went in support of GEORGE. Separate accounts had The Company of operation were considered a success attached.	
CARENCY SECTOR	27	-	99 M.G.C. relieves by 1st of A Coy. who took over toilers as occupied by 99 M.G.Coy. B guns took up reserve position in MAISTRE ad BASQUE line.	
CAMBLAIN L'ABBÉ.	28		H.Q. at CAMBLAIN L'ABBÉ. with 2 sections out of the line.	
	29		} Nothing to report.	
	30			

99th Inf.Bde.
2nd Div.

WAR DIARY

99th MACHINE GUN COMPANY.

J U L Y

1 9 1 6

Army Form C. 2118.

WAR DIARY

99th Inf. Bde. M.G. Coy.

6/8/16.

Herewith war diary
of 99th M.G. Coy for
July 1916.
This diary has not been
kept & entered up daily
after July 14th by the
2nd O.C. Officer of Coy as
2nd O.C. has been
conjured from notes
given him and currently
ever by one officer left
of twenty six the others
& many N.C.Os & men
having been killed wounded
in DELVILLE WOOD

Noel Cox Capt
Comdg 99 M.G. Coy

Army Form C. 2118.

Vol 4 2/99

99th Machine Gun Coy.

Place	Date	Hour	Summary of Events and Information	Remarks and references to Appendices
CAMBLAIN L'ABBÉ	1/7		~~Heavy enemy gun fire~~ heard from early morning. Very heavy artillery activity S. of ARRAS	
"	2		Heavy gun fire to the South.	
"	3		Nothing to report.	
"	4		Relieved 48th Bde. M.G.C. in BRETHENCOURT SECTION and in Syms. Nil Section company hdqtrs. O.O. regarding relief in Appendix	App 1.
"	5th/16th/		Records lost. No information found relating to moves of offrs etc.	
"	17th		This company was relieved by the 140 M.G. Coy on night 17/18 and returned to rest billets at CABARET ROUGE (Bde operation order lost)	
HERMAIN	18th		Left CAMBLAIN L'ABBÉ and proceeded to HERMAIN	J.S.
"	19th		Six reinforcements joined from Base.	
DEVIEL	20th		Left HERMAIN for DEVIEL and entrained	
MORLANCOURT	21st		arrived at AMIENS and marched to MORLANCOURT.	

Army Form C. 2118.

WAR DIARY
or
INTELLIGENCE SUMMARY.
(Erase heading not required.)

99th Machine Gun Company

Place	Date	Hour	Summary of Events and Information	Remarks and references to Appendices
	1916			
MORLANCOURT	July 22nd		Nothing to report.	
"	23rd		Inspection of the Company by O.C. 99th Inf. Bde.	
HAULTE	24th		Left MORLANCOURT and camped at HAULTE. Took over billets from 26th Machine Gun Coy.	
MONTAUBAN	25th		Left HAULTE and moved to MONTAUBAN.	
DELVILLE WOOD	26/27		Brigade Op. Order for attack on DELVILLE WOOD Cr̄est. An extract of this order is as follows:—	
			R.P. MONTAUBAN. TRENCH MAP 1/20000	
			99th M.G.C. Operation Order No. 15. July 26th 1916.	
			(1) The 99th Inf. Bde. are attacking DELVILLE WOOD at 7.10 a.m. to-morrow.	
			(2) Artillery barrage commences at 6.10 a.m. on 27th inst. and will last one hour before lifting onto German second line. Barrage of second line will last one hour and lift N. of wood.	R.S.
			(3) 1st Royal Berkshire Regt. are Battalion consolidating Battalion behind 23rd Royal Fusiliers and 1st Kings Royal Rifle Corps.	

Army Form C. 2118.

WAR DIARY
or
INTELLIGENCE SUMMARY

(Erase heading not required.)

99th Machine-Gun Coy

July 1916

Place	Date 1916	Hour	Summary of Events and Information	Remarks and references to Appendices
DENVILLE WOOD	26/27		Op. Nois. contd.	

(4) No 1 Section and Sec Co act in support of the two centre Companies of 1/R.B.R.
No 2 Section in support of the right company
No 3   "   in support of the left company
No 4   "   in reserve

(5) O.C. Company rode up with the reserve section (No 4) and Operations as copied from section commander's reports.

No 1 Section

Went into action on it "WILLOW" (1/K.R.R.C.) One gun did not come into action. 3 guns were close together in the centre of the line held by the 1/K.R.R.C. These guns fired approx-imately 13500 rounds S.A.A. The Germans appeared in ambling formation and extended order and about 200 also came over from right some disorganised. The whole of the section came under very heavy shell fire, both in wood and in reserve. Both and [unclear] and fired.

No 2 Section

Went into action on its "ASH" (1/Royal Berks.) One gun went into front line on it 1/K.R.R.C., guarding the right flank. Engaged German reinforcements. Firing 1500 rounds S.A.A. and 500 rounds in repelling the rifle bombing attack. Gun came out of the line having [unclear]

WAR DIARY or INTELLIGENCE SUMMARY

Army Form C. 2118.

Place	Date	Hour	Summary of Events and Information	Remarks and references to Appendices
DELVILLE WOOD	26/27		Operations contd. No more ammunition. 2 guns stopped in support in trench in wood and did not fire, being in support. All guns came under very heavy shell fire. **103 Section** Went into action with "BEECH" Co. 2nd Royal Fusiliers. Prior to reaching posn. Pearsons trench, were in touch with "BEECH" Guarding Ken Lft with each other. One gun with "BEECH" Guarding Ken Lft flank did not fire. 3 guns close fire there with 1 Royal Berks. Here latter fired about 600 rounds sqn. on the Germans who appeared to be determinedly massing and arising. All guns came under very heavy arty today and bombarder fire Communication was impossible to maintain owing to the nature of the shell fire. 11 o'h section were in reserve. Received orders from Capt. Banks, O.C. 95, sects. on Tuesday to move up into the front line and proceed onto the original post. There was kept up their continually on the German reinforcements and counter attacks. Some extensive cuts made by very heavy shell fire. Reasons Communication appearances to the front line were extremely difficult to keep up owing to the nature of the hostile fire.	P.T.O.

Army Form C. 2118.

WAR DIARY
or
INTELLIGENCE SUMMARY

(Erase heading not required.)

89th Machine Gun Coy.

July 1916.

Place	Date 1916	Hour	Summary of Events and Information	Remarks and references to Appendices
CORBAY	28th		Moved to CORBAY after the action nr SART 28/29. Casualties from 26/7 – 31/7	*Indemnity attached
	27th		Killed — Offrs. O.R. / Wounded — Offrs. O.R. / Missing — Offrs. O.R.	
			CAPT. GRANT 13* 2nd Lt. HEAL 9 Nil Nil	
			LT. CRAWFORD " MORITZ	
	28th		5* " FLETCHER BARRETT 17 " 7	
			" FRENCH 2	
	29th		Nil " FERRIER 3 " 1	
	31st			
	Total		2 Offrs. 18 5 Offrs. 21 Nil 8	
BROMFAY FARM.	31st	9pm	Moved to BROMFAY FARM for rest.	

99th Brigade.
2nd Division.

99th BRIGADE MACHINE GUN COMPANY

AUGUST 1916.

Army Form C. 2118.

WAR DIARY
or
INTELLIGENCE SUMMARY.

(Erase heading not required.)

SECRET

WAR DIARY

OF

99th MACHINE GUN COMPANY

from

AUGIST — AUG 31ST 1916

WAR DIARY

or

INTELLIGENCE SUMMARY.

(Erase heading not required.)

Place	Date	Hour	Summary of Events and Information	Remarks and references to Appendices
In the field	August 1st		Owing to casualties of officers the machine gun company was split up into subsections and two guns sent to each of the 4 Battalions to be under their direct orders. Three 8 guns were sent in to DELVILLE WOOD when they were under the Command of Lieut. Col. BARKER. The remainder of the company went back into reserve at 7.29063 + The Teams in the line consisted of 1 NCO + 4 men. Ref 62D NE.	
	August 2nd		Capt A.P. Snell officer commanding 99th M.G. Coy, Yr A.K. Day. Lewis is appointed 2nd in Command. Lts Cornwell, Lindsay Wall, Hamilton & Champion reported for duty with the Company at 4/3 pm. The sections of the Company in reserve were being reorganised.	U.K. Army H
	August 3rd		The eight Vickers gun teams, which were in the trenches an attaches to battalions, were relieved this afternoon by 8 fresh teams for those in reserve. This relief left reserve camp at 3.15 pm and relief was completed by midnight.	
	August 4th		News reached Company HQ at noon that one gun in DELVILLE WOOD had been knocked out and one Corporal wounded; A relieving party of 1 Corpl + 1 private was sent up at once to take the place of those casualties.	

Army Form C. 2118.

WAR DIARY
or
INTELLIGENCE SUMMARY.
(Erase heading not required.)

Instructions regarding War Diaries and Intelligence Summaries are contained in F. S. Regs., Part II. and the Staff Manual respectively. Title pages will be prepared in manuscript.

Place	Date	Hour	Summary of Events and Information	Remarks and references to Appendices
In the Field	Aug 4th		Brigade operation order No 50 dated August 4th 1916 ordered the machine guns at present in the trenches to be relieved by the 51st Machine Gun Coy. The teams were to accompany the 1st Royal Berkshires as far as junction with main road S OF CARNOY where they would be met by guides to conduct them to where they would join the remainder of the Company. At 5 pm the remainder of the Company were ordered to move to HAPPY VALLEY and bivouac there for the night of the 4th-5th. They arrived in their Brigade area quarters at 6.15 pm. Draft of 18 ORs arrived at 5 pm from base.	A.K.Day. Lieut. ft
	August 5th		Relief of gun teams (8) from DELVILLE WOOD was completed at 12.15 pm to-day and the company was reported all present at HAPPY VALLEY at 6 pm. L.2.d.49. Ref 57 C NW 1/10000 REF. MONTAUBAN 1/20000.	
	August 6th		Company still bivouaced in HAPPY VALLEY.	
	August 7th		Company still bivouaced in HAPPY VALLEY.	
	August 8th		Operation order No 66 by Brigade ordered the 99th Machine Gun Coy to move to SAND PIT VALLEY to arrive there by 3.30 pm. A billeting party of 1 officer + 4 ORs met the	

WAR DIARY
or
INTELLIGENCE SUMMARY
(Erase heading not required.)

Army Form C. 2118.

Place	Date	Hour	Summary of Events and Information	Remarks and references to Appendices
	August 8		Staff Captain E.24.6.6.9. came 1/2000. at 11AM. The Transport was ordered to stand fast. The Company paraded at 1.45 ready to move off at 2.0 pm. After orders were sent to bring our Transport with the Company. On arrival at 3 pm at SAND PIT VALLEY the Company after we were going to relieve had had orders that they were to remain another night in their present bivouac. The 99th Machine Gun Company finally bivouaced at 7.30.p.m.	
	August 9th		Company in same bivouac as above	
	August 10th		Same as above; a draft of 1 Officer and 18 ORs reported at 9.30 pm from base.	
	August 11th		Orders from 67 Bde Brigade ordered the 99th M.G. Coy to accompany the 99th Inf. Bde to MERICOURT L'ABBE' via MEAULTE Lower road on VILLE SUR ANCRE. Starting point of Brigade was E.15.A Cross Roads CARCAILLOT and the Company passed it at 1.56 pm. 2nd Lt Champion and 4 ORs reported to Staff Captain at 11 AM starting point for the purpose of billetting. Transport horses and all transport vehicles assembled under 99th Bde Transport Officer at CROSS TRACKS L.1.a.5.1. at 11.30 AM & proceeded to DAOURS Route MORLANCOURT - K87.d.50 - T17.d.1.1. main BRAY - CORBIE road. On arrival at DAOURS it came under the orders of Lt Col E.W. Brown DSO Comdg 2nd Div. Train.	AK.Day. Run. 2ff

1577 Wt.W.10791/1773 500,000 1/15 D. D. & L. A.D.S.S./Forms/C. 2118.

Army Form C. 2118.

WAR DIARY
or
INTELLIGENCE SUMMARY.
(Erase heading not required.)

Place	Date	Hour	Summary of Events and Information	Remarks and references to Appendices
In the field	August 11th		Sufficient Camp kettles were to be taken to enable the 14th Inst. Packs were to be carried by all ranks but at 11 a.m. orders were cancelled & we received Lorry to take all packs and stores. The Company paraded at 1.15 pm ready to march off at 1.30 pm, he arrived in our new billets at 5.30 pm; they were billeted round about J.3.d.4.2.	A.K. Day-Lewis 2/Lt
	August 12th		The Company received the following orders. Ref 1/100,000. The 99th Machine Gun Company would entrain from MERICOURT L'ABBE to hurry to SALEUX; The Company would detrain at SALEUX and would proceed to billets to VAUX EN AMIENOIS. At SALEUX lorries would take men packs and a certain number of men to billets, the remainder would march. Upto the time order to Entrain at 3AM the final order came that the Company were to entrain at 7AM.	REF. AMIENS 1/100,000 17
	Aug 13th		The Company paraded at 6.15 Am ready to march off at 6.30 AM 13/8/16 and proceeded to HERICOURT LABBE STATION. 2nd Lt Champion and 4 NCOs met the Staff Captain at time arriving at 7AM. Each man carried 1 days ration in haversack. The Company entrained at 9.10 AM and detrained at SALEUX at 1.45 PM. No Conveyances Carts be found for the men so they started off at 2.30 pm to march to VAUX EN AMIENOIS via the OUTSKIRTS OF AMIENS. They arrived in their new billets at 7.30 pm	

WAR DIARY
or
INTELLIGENCE SUMMARY.
(Erase heading not required.)

Army Form C. 2118.

Place	Date	Hour	Summary of Events and Information	Remarks and references to Appendices
? to ?	Aug 15th Aug 15		A draft of 16 men arrived from 5th R of R.B. Company in billets in VAUX EN AMIENOIS and 50% were granted leave to AMIENS.	A.M. Day Lewis 2/L
	Aug 16th		Same as above.	
			The 99th Machine Gun company received the following orders:— Brigade Operation Order No 70 dated August 16th 1916. The Company will move to AREA C tomorrow. The starting point will be STA (1 mile S of FLESSELLES) All the transport were to follow the Company and the Company were to follow the 13th K.R.R. The Company paraded by sections in their own billets at 2.15 pm and moved transport up in "Company in line." opposite No 2 sections billets at 2.35 pm ready to march off. Packs were carried on the man. Lt Champion and 2 NCO's met the Staff Captain in the middle of WARGNIES at 2 pm for the purpose of billeting.	
	Aug 17th		REF MAP LENS 17 1/100,000 The Company received orders to move this day to A Area = 99th Inf Bde Operation order No 71 stated that the starting point was X ROADS 1½ miles south of GEZAINCOURT. The Company were to pass that point at 10.17 AM. The Company V in VALHEUREUX, and the Company marched off at 9 AM. The Company arrived in their billets at 11.30 AM. Lt Champion and 2 NCO's reported to the Staff Captain at the MAIRIE at 11.30 AM for the purpose of billeting.	

Army Form C. 2118.

WAR DIARY
or
INTELLIGENCE SUMMARY.
(Erase heading not required.)

Place	Date	Hour	Summary of Events and Information	Remarks and references to Appendices
In the field	Aug 18th		99 Inf Bde Operation orders No 72 dated 17/8/16. stated that we were to move on the 18th from our present billets to VAUCHELLES LES AUTHIE. The starting point of the Brigade was X ROADS ¼ mile East of STA at South end of GEZAINCOURT (G.3.c.2.q) & the company was to pass it at 7.3 AM. The Company paraded at 6.30 ready to march off at 6.45 AM. Owing to movements of Other Brigades across our route, the march was considerably delayed & the Company finally arrived in their new billets at 1 pm.	Artillery form up. REF MAP 57D NE 1/40,000
	Aug 19th		The Company received orders that they would not move from their billets today, but received the following orders for the 20th Aug. 1916. Operation Order No 73 - 19.8.16 by 99th Inf Bde stated that the Company would move with the rest of the Brigade to Billets in BUS-LES-ARTOIS to-morrow. The starting point would be road junction T.16.a.96 (East of AUTHIE) and the company were to pass it at 2.31 pm.	
	Aug 20th		The Company paraded outside their billets at 1.30 pm & moved off at 1145 pm. Mr Champion & 2 NCO's proceeded to meet the Staff Captain at the MAIRIE at BUS LES ARTOIS at 12 Noon. The Company arrived in their new billets by 4 pm.	

WAR DIARY
or
INTELLIGENCE SUMMARY.

(Erase heading not required.)

Army Form C. 2118.

Place	Date	Hour	Summary of Events and Information	Remarks and references to Appendices
Field	Aug 20th (contd)		The following order was received from Brigade at 11.45 AM to-day — 99th Brigade Operation Order No 74 dated 20th Aug 1916 — The Company in conjunction with the rear of the brigade would relieve the 2nd GUARDS BRIGADE in the left Section of the divisional line on 21/8/16 as per attached March Table. All details of relief were to be arranged by direct communication between O's C units concerned. The First line transport were to be located at T.8.a.2. No transport was to be on the road BUS - LES ARTOIS — COUN between the hours of 9.0 AM & 11.30 AM on 21)8)16. The line would be taken over as at present held. The 99th Machine Gun Company were to move from BUS LES ARTOIS to relieve the 2nd GUARDS Machine Gun Company and the route was to be as follows. Road Junction (T.33.b.09.) Road Junction (T.27.b.94.) Cross roads (T.23.a.76) - road junction T.18.c.68. Guides would be at T.15.c.68 at 6.30 AM. at which hour Sections were to move at 5 minute interval.	A.M. Dauphine Yt
	Aug 21st		The Company paraded at 4.45 AM ready to march off at 5 AM. Guides met the Company at the above place at 6.30 AM & the Sections proceeded independently as far as Hebuterne Village when the limbers were unloaded & the Teams, chained to the Trenches, were met by guides to conduct them, while the remaining Guns & their Teams	

WAR DIARY
INTELLIGENCE SUMMARY

Army Form C. 2118.

Place	Date	Hour	Summary of Events and Information	Remarks and references to Appendices
In the Field	Aug 21st (cont)		proceeded to billets in the Village of HEBUTERNE. Company Head quarters were situated at K15 b.64. (HEBUTERNE VILLAGE). 2/Lt Champion with 4 guns & 4 teams (of 1 NCO + 8 men) relieved the four guns & teams on the right of the Sector taken over. The position of the guns were from No1. K22 C41. No2. K22 C26 No3 K22 b43 No4 K22 d36. These positions were manned by teams Section 4. 2/Lt Gordon with two teams (1 NCO 2 men) from Section 2 were taken by guide to relieve the two middle emplacements; their position on the map being K22 A.49 & K22 a.25. 2/Lt Lindsay and 4 teams (1 NCO + 3 men) from Section 1 proceeded to take over the 4 left positions. The positions of these were ("Botha") K16 a.52; (Relieving) K16 a.85 (Oliver de Chosin) K16 b.18; ("Allenis") K16 d.56. This relief was completed by 9.45 A.M. In addition to their position 2/Lt Champion made up three of this guns every night to a forward position in Wrangle Avenue K23 a 92.	A.K. Dey. Lieut. y+
	Aug 22nd		Nothing to report. On the night of the 22nd–23rd 12 heavy mortars shell fell near the forward position (K23 a 92) but did no damage	REF MAP 57 D NE 1/20,000
	Aug 23rd		Nothing to report; everything was quiet.	
	Aug 24th		On relieving the Guards Machine Gun Coy the position in Wrangle Avenue (K23 a 92) was merely an open emplacement with no roofing to it. To-day this sap was made from main communication trench to Emplacement. Work was also commenced on a dugout for that position	

WAR DIARY
~~INTELLIGENCE~~ SUMMARY
(Erase heading not required.)

Army Form C. 2118.

Place	Date	Hour	Summary of Events and Information	Remarks and references to Appendices
In the field	Aug 25th		Everything quiet; work proceeds on Orange Avenue position.	
	Aug 26th		All quiet; work was commenced on three new positions; they were situated at 1 (Kronprinz) K23.a.52.7 (Pasteur) K17.c.4.z; 3 Bugeaud (K17.c.4.z). These were all to have 20 feet dugouts with open emplacements. Work is being carried on both by daylight in the above positions as well as on Orange Avenue.	
	Aug 27		All quiet.	REF MAP 57D NE 1/20,000.
	Aug 28th		To-day we were ordered to observe for gaps in enemies barbed wire & if they showed & open, we were to open a steady fire by night on those gaps. No gaps were seen. Work continued on the 4 forward positions.	All day fine & hot.
	Aug 29th		Bombardment on our right was extremely violent but our sector was quiet all day.	
	Aug 30		This morning we were ordered to prepare our guns to open fire by night on the communication and other trenches belonging to the Boches. It rained heavily all day which resulted in it being very quiet, & our guns did not fire by night	

Army Form C. 2118.

WAR DIARY
or
INTELLIGENCE SUMMARY.
(Erase heading not required.)

Instructions regarding War Diaries and Intelligence Summaries are contained in F. S. Regs., Part II. and the Staff Manual respectively. Title pages will be prepared in manuscript.

Place	Date	Hour	Summary of Events and Information	Remarks and references to Appendices
In the field	Aug 3rd		All remained quiet during the day. The weather was fine and great aeroplane activity was being carried on over our trenches.	

Rpt Innes Cpt
a.c. 99th M.L. By
1/9/16

99th Brigade.
2nd Divison

99th MACHINE GUN COMPANY

SEPTEMBER 1 9 1 6

A/ DAA
3rd Echelon

Herewith Copy of War Diary
for September

Hawkins L
99th M.G. Co

Oct 1st 16

Army Form C. 2118.

Vol 6. 99

WAR DIARY or INTELLIGENCE SUMMARY

(Erase heading not required.)

99th Machine-Gun Company

Instructions regarding War Diaries and Intelligence Summaries are contained in F. S. Regs., Part II. and the Staff Manual respectively. Title Pages will be prepared in manuscript.

Place	Date 1916	Hour	Summary of Events and Information	Remarks and references to Appendices
HÉBUTERNE Sector	1/9	9pm	Fire was brought to bear from 3 guns on the enemy's arc by the artillery at K17 b 0.5 & K17 d 1.6. (Ref. HÉBUTERNE 1/10.000). Quiet 24 hours.	
"	2/9		Machine gun dug-outs in front line at K23 a 4.3, K17 c 0.2, K17 c 2.8 & K23 b 0.2 have been dug to a depth of 15'. Fire was directed on gp at K17 d 1.6 during the night.	
"	3/9		A hostile bombardment with lachrymatory shells lasting from 9pm till 2am night 3/4 chiefly in the S91.27 – 9U – 3015 area. 2nd Lt. G.D. Hamilton & 4 O.R.'s proceeded to a dump at CAMIERS. 2nd Lt. Cornwall returned from dump at CAMIERS.	
"	4/9		Gas was discharged on the 9p to the front by our troops.	
"	5/9.		Nothing to report. Quiet 24 hours.	
"	6/9	3pm	2nd Lt. Champion (190th Section) returned by 2nd Lt. Harris (1903) in V1, V2, V6 & V7 ASHA sector. 2nd Lt. Lindsay relieved by 2nd Lt. Cornwall in V12, V13, V14 & ABLAIN sector and 2nd Lt. London relieved by 2 Reserve teams of No 2 & teams under 2nd Lt. Section in V8 & V19	

WAR DIARY
or
INTELLIGENCE SUMMARY

(Erase heading not required.)

Army Form C. 2118.

92nd Machine Gun Company

Place	Date 1916	Hour	Summary of Events and Information	Remarks and references to Appendices
HÉBUTERNE Sector	7/9		The following changes have been made in the positions of certain M.G. Guns at follows:- (a) Guns in K16 c 5.0 moved to K16 c 2.5 (CEMETERY)	Ref. HÉBUTERNE 1/10.000
"			(b) Guns K16 b 1.5 to K16 a 9.5.6.5 (c) Gun K22 c 3.4 to K23 c 0.1 (d) Guns K22 c 3.6 to K23 a 7.2. In addition 2 more guns occupied positions in K16 c 9.1 and K16 b 8.5 respectively making a total of 12 guns in the line & 4 in reserve	
"	8/9		Nothing to report. Resisted 24 hours	
"	9/9		Work in the front line dug-outs has been continuing daily & nightly at K28 a 4.3, K17 c 4.2, K17 c 2.5 & K23 b 0.2, a depth of 25 feet reached including 8 feet passage to dug-out tunnel.	
"	10/9		Nothing to report.	
"	11/9		Nothing to report.	
"	12/9	50 m	HÉBUTERNE was shelled for about 15 mins. chiefly shrapnel	
"	13/9		Between 9pm and dawn guns V.6, V.7, V.8, V.13, were fired at intervals during the night on the German trenches & communications south to K23 b 5.5. Particular attention was paid to gap out by the following between K17 central & K17 d 1.7	

WAR DIARY or INTELLIGENCE SUMMARY

Army Form C. 2118.

Place	Date	Hour	Summary of Events and Information	Remarks and references to Appendices
HÉBUTERNE Sector.	14/9		The same guns fired between 9 p.m. & dawn as the German ones as on the 13th inst. Quiet 24 hours.	
"	15/9		A successful raid was carried out by the 22nd Regt at positions from K.17.d.17. to K.17.b.20. The following machine guns assisted materially and fired as follows from 9.30 pm to 11.50 p.m. (a) V.14a. a German communication trench from K.17.b.3.8. to K.17.b.9.8. (b) 101's from junction of Pinhon road + Fonky front line to K.11.d.1.0. (c) German communication trench 200' east of THE POINT. (d) V.7 from K.23.b.3.7. to THE POINT. (e) V.6 from K.17.d.1.0. to K.23.b.3.7. (f) All guns except V.V.8 & V.16.a commenced firing guns at 12.36 am on same target but with 200' extra elevation. V.8 & V.16.a fired on the same elevation. The ranges varied from 900' to 1000'. (g) All guns fired till the last moment of the raid.	
"	16/9		Work has been continuing daily urgently on the new front line dug outs at K.23.a.4.3, K.17.c.4.2, K.17.c.25. K.K.25.6.02. The majority of dug outs complete, 8 feet of 2nd entrance to army to carry to onwards dug outs completed.	

WAR DIARY
or
INTELLIGENCE SUMMARY

(Erase heading not required.)

9th Machine Gun Coy

Instructions regarding War Diaries and Intelligence Summaries are contained in F.S. Regs., Part II and the Staff Manual respectively. Title Pages will be prepared in manuscript.

Place	Date	Hour	Summary of Events and Information	Remarks and references to Appendices
HEBUTERNE	17/9 1916		Nothing to report. Quiet 24 hours.	REF HEBUTERNE 1:10,000
"	18/9		Approved raid by 1/KRRc postponed on account of wet weather. Reps at K23d 84 being kept open by M.G. fire from K23 & 1.0.	
"	19/9		Nos 3 & 2 Sections were relieved by reserve teams from HEBUTERNE Ref. 99th Bde. Op Order No 82. The following reliefs took place.	
"	20/9		(a) O.C. 117 K.M.G.Coy relieved Nos 2 & 4 Sections as follows.	
			(b) O.C. Nos 3 K.M.G. Batty. relieved teams at V.12, V.13, & V.14.	
			(c) 1 Sect. 117 K.M.G.Coy relieved No 3 Section in V1, V2, V6 & V7.	
			(d) Teams in V.8, V.9, V.10 remained in the line under 2 KRR Lindsay.	
			(e) Teams in ASHEUIN & V.15 remained in the line under 2nd Lt. Lindsay.	
			(f) 3 teams of 99th M.G.Coy remained in reserve at HEBUTERNE.	
			(g) Nos 2 & 4 Sections personnel remained under O.C. 117 K.M.G.Coy.	
			Nos 1 & 3 Sections on relief left HEBUTERNE with Coy Coy H.Q. at 2 p.m. & marched via COUIN - ST LEGER to BOIS DU WARNIMONT	
			and billeted there.	
BOIS DU WARNIMONT	21/9.		Nos 2 & 4 Sections undergoing training.	

Army Form C. 2118.

WAR DIARY
or
INTELLIGENCE SUMMARY

(Erase heading not required.)   99ᵗʰ M.G. Coy

Instructions regarding War Diaries and Intelligence Summaries are contained in F. S. Regs., Part II. and the Staff Manual respectively. Title Pages will be prepared in manuscript.

Place	Date	Hour	Summary of Events and Information	Remarks and references to Appendices
BOIS DU WARNIMONT	22/9		Nothing to report. Training	
"	23/9		2 n.c.o. Hamilton returned from CAMIERS	
"	24/9		Nothing to report	
"	25/9		Recce was made by 1/KRRC. Plans were made for the N.G. in connection with 1/KRRC & returned to O.C. 117 & 119 Inf. Bde. 2 @ guns from 99th find as follows.	
REF. HEBUTERNE 57.D.V.S.	26/9 11.00 am.		(b) Temporary Position in K 23 c 9 c. from K 23 d 7. to K 29 b 3.6. Gap at K17 b 0.1. from the gap to K17 b 0.1. Lt. Day - Lewis proceeded on leave to the UK. Orders were received to be ready to move on 24 hours notice.	
"	27/9		Company ordered to be ready to move at 4 hours notice.	
"	28/9		37 O.R. supplies to the 2nd Battalion of the Coy. ordered to be returned to base.	
"	29/9		11 O.R.'s & 4 sections relieved by Nos. 1 & 3 sections at 12 noon in the HEBUTERNE sector. 2 n.c.o. Crowhell also was to be relieved for us. but. Hamilton stayed in the line owing to the latter officer being admitted into the ???	

2449 Wt. W14957/M90 750,000 1/16 J.B.C. & A. Forms/C.2118/12.

WAR DIARY or INTELLIGENCE SUMMARY

Army Form C. 2118.

(Erase heading not required.) 99th Machine Gun Coy.

Place	Date	Hour	Summary of Events and Information	Remarks and references to Appendices
COURCELLES AU BOIS	2/9/		99th Inf. Bde. Instructions No.17 received ordering this unit to take over gun positions between K.34 & 9.0 to JOHN COPSE (Ref. HÉBUTERNE 1.10.000). The Company moved from BOIS DE WARNIMONT at 10 a.m. & marched via BUS-LES-ARTOIS — BERTRANCOURT to COURCELLES. Company H.Q. returned at J.29.B.30 via two. 2nd Lt Champion & 27 O.R. (4 guns) between K.34.6.20 & K.29.a. 1 Sect 117 M.G. Coy (4 guns) between K.28.C. & K.29.a. one gun in K.27.d. Relief completed at 5.30 p.m. 2nd Lt. Harwood & 24 O.R. of No.2 Sect. relieved 1 Sect. 116 M.G. Coy. (4 guns) between K.34.6.20 & K.27.d. S.O. Relief completed at 6 p.m. 2 Remaining sections (8 guns) in HÉBUTERNE sect. between HÉBUTERNE & JOHN COPSE. Gaps were kept open by M.G. fire from M.S.A.T. at K.35.C.44.—C4.7. K.35.a.2.1. K.35.C.44.—C4.7 & K.35.a.2.1.	R.J. Smith Capt. OC 99th M.G. Coy.

2449 Wt. W14957/M90 750,000 1/16 J.B.C. & A. Forms/C.2118/12.

99th Brigade.
2nd Division.

99th MACHINE GUN COMPANY

OCTOBER 1916

99th M.G.C.
Vol 7

INTELLIGENCE SUMMARY

Place	Date	Hour	Summary of Events and Information	Remarks and references to Appendices
Oct 1st COURCELLES			The Company Head Quarters are at Courcelles, and 8 guns are situated in the HEBUTERNE Sector and, 8 guns in the EGG ST – WATLING ST Sector. REF HEBUTERNE 1/10000 TRENCH MAP. BEAUMONT	
	2nd Oct		The 99th Machine Gun Company received to-day Operation Order No 84 of 99th Inf Bde stating that the Brigade was taking over new Frontage from F.O. of 116 Inf Bde to-morrow Oct 3rd. Relief to WATLING STREET from the 116 Inf Bde. O.C. 99th Machine Gun Company was to have be completed by 3 p.m. at 14th Royal Sussex Bn. H.Q. at 8.45 A.M. To-morrow 3rd in order to reconnaître the line and to arrange all necessary details and hour of relief. 99th Machine Coy H.Q. were to move from COURCELLES to MAILLY on 3rd OCTOBER. The Machine Guns of the 6th Inf Bde at present in the line were to be replaced by those of this Company, whereas the guns of the 6th Inf Bde were to remain in and at present in the line. It was understood that the Guns of the 99th Inf Bde at present in the HEBUTERNE SECTION would be relieved on the 4th October and that on relief they	All by Jun. Hy

INTELLIGENCE SUMMARY

(Erase heading not required.)

Summaries are contained in F.S. Regs., Part II. and the Staff Manual respectively. Title Pages will be prepared in manuscript.

Place	Date	Hour	Summary of Events and Information	Remarks and references to Appendices
COURCELLES	2nd		would return to the 99th Machine Gun Company	
MAILLY	3rd		This Company moved in to Head Quarters at MAILLY to-day. Three guns from the HEBUTERNE section were relieved to-day & have joined the H.Q. of the 99th Machine Gun Coy.	
MAILLY	4th		The remaining five guns from the HEBUTERNE section returned to the Company, and the 3 guns which rejoined the Company yesterday were sent up to the line under Lt Lindsay.	
MAILLY	5th		The five remaining guns left at H.Q. of 99th Machine Gun Coy were sent up into the line. Orders have received to-day that the 99th Inf Bde were to be relieved by the 5th Inf. Bde. on the sixth. REF. HEBUTERNE 1/10000 TRENCH MAP. BEAUMONT 1/10000 99th Inf Bde Order No 85 dated 4th Oct. 1916. 99th Inf Bde will move into the area vacated by the 5th Inf Bde; the 99th Machine Gun Company will occupy billets in MAILLY-MAILLET VILLAGE.	

INTELLIGENCE SUMMARY

(Erase heading not required.)

Summaries are contained in F.S. Regs., Part II. and the Staff Manual respectively. Title Pages will be prepared in manuscript.

Place	Date	Hour	Summary of Events and Information	Remarks and references to Appendices
MAILLY	5th		Billeting party from 99th Machine Gun Company will meet guides of 5th Inf. Bde at 99th Bde HQrs at 10 A.M. 6/10/16. Machine Gun Company will make their own relief arrangements and guides. Rendezvous & we here to commence our relief at 9.30 A.M. Completion of relief will be reported to Brigade Headquarters.	OK Roy Maj. T
MAILLY	6th		In accordance with the above operation order, the 99th Machine Gun Coy was relieved this morning by the 5th Machine Gun Coy and remained in huts in MAILLY.	
"	7th		Extract of 99th Inf. Bde Order No 86 dated 7.10.16 and received today. REF MAP, Sheet 57C. The 99th Inf. Bde will move tomorrow in accordance with attached March table. The 99th Machine Gun Company are to move on the 8.10.16 & pass the starting point at Cross roads at P12.C at 1.50 p.m. The route to be through FORCEVILLE, ACHEUX, LEALVILLERS and the dismounted RAINCHEVAL. Billeting parties are to meet the Staff Captain at RAINCHEVAL CHURCH at 11 A.M.	

Place	Date	Hour	Summary of Events and Information	Remarks and references to Appendices
MAILLY	7th OCT.		2/Lt G.D. HAMILTON was to-day evacuated to England, sick.	
RAINCHEVAL	8th		In accordance with above orders and taking the above route, the Company paraded outside their billets at 1.30 p.m. ready to pass starting point at P.12.c at 1.50 p.m. The Company arrived here in billets at 5.30 p.m.	
"	9th		Capt. Snell received orders to proceed to CROSS ROADS at O.19.C and meet the Brigadier with a view to reconnoitring the ground traversing O.19. + O.13. for the purpose of attack in a Northerly direction from the crossing at O.19.C. (REF 57c MAP 1/40000)	Attn Bay-Paris 1/40
"	10th		Capt. Snell, Lt Dowtown, Lt Lindsay & Lt Cornwall started off to O.19.C to survey the ground in O.19.+13. in the morning, and at 2 p.m. Capt Snell, Lt Day-Lewis, Lt Champion & 2/Lt Haward proceeded there + met the Brigadier + discussed the plan of the attack, afterwards they proceeded across the attacking area	

INTELLIGENCE SUMMARY

(Erase heading not required.)

Place	Date	Hour	Summary of Events and Information	Remarks and references to Appendices
BAINCHEVAL	OCT 11th		A Divisional Practice attack was held to-day. The 99th Machine Gun Company paraded outside their billets at 8.30 + marched off at 8.55 in rear of the 1st K.R.R. so as to form the CROSS ROADS at O.19.C at 9.25 AM. The Scheme of the attack was as follows:— REF. MAP. (TRENCH) PUISIEUX-AU-MONT 1:5000.— It was proposed that the 2nd Division in conjunction with the 2nd Division on would attack the SERRE position in 4 stages up to and as far as the Sunken road at L20.C central along a line known as the BROWN LINE to L26.C.6.6. thence to L32.b.4.4. thence to L31.d.50. The 5th + 6th Brigades were to capture the all the front line German defences as far as a line — THE GREEN LINE —, shelving from K36.A.2.9. to K36.d.0.9. After a halt on this line the 5th + 6th Brigades were to advance, in conjunction with the 2nd Division, on their left, and capture the — YELLOW LINE — from K36.a.7.9. thence to K36.a.2.5 + then along to K35.d.0.4. Along road to K36.a.9.2, thence to K36.a.2.5 + then along for the capture of a line — THE BLUE LINE — The 99th Inf. Bde were responsible for the capture of a line — THE BLUE LINE — extending from K.36.b.7.5 to K36.c.5.0. They were then to push forward	

Place	Date	Hour	Summary of Events and Information	Remarks and references to Appendices
RAINCHEVAL	Oct 11th		and occupy the Sunken road – from L.26.d.20 to L.31.d.5p. Finally the 99th Inf. Bde. were to front forward and capture a line – THE BROWN LINE – extending from L.26.c.8.1. to L.32.A.53. Thence to L.31.d.5.0. The Divisional bi-day was carried out on ground marked out by tape & represented the actual lines which were the various objectives in the attack. The BROWN LINE was emitted bi-day & no parade was called on the Capture of the BLUE LINE. The 5th & 6th Brigades were formed up in imaginary assembly trenches the leading lines not being more forward than the tapes marking the British Front line. The 99th Inf. Bde formed up in rear just in front of BOIS GREFTEL at O.25.c.99 (Ref Map.57c.1:40,000) Zero hour was 10.30 A.M. when a Very light was fired by the 15th Inf. Bde HQ. The 22nd & 23rd Royal Fusiliers were our front attacking line with the 1st KRR's & 1st Royal Berkshires composed the second line.	

INTELLIGENCE SUMMARY

(Erase heading not required.)

Summaries are contained in F.S. Regs., Part II. and the Staff Manual respectively. Title Pages will be prepared in manuscript.

Place	Date	Hour	Summary of Events and Information	Remarks and references to Appendices
RAINCHEVAL	11th		The 99th Machine Gun Coy Guns were distributed as follows – 4 guns to each of the leading Battalions and 2 sent to the rear Battalions while one complete section was kept in reserve. The most suitable method for the Machine guns to advance was in the same formation as that of the infantry and to advance with their last wave.	Watson Lt/A
RAINCHEVAL	12th		A Brigade practice attack took place to-day exactly similar to the above programme.	
RAINCHEVAL	13th		A second Divisional practice took place to-day. The 99th Inf Bde were formed up in rear of CREFTELWOOD (O.25.d.40.) Ref Map 57C 1/40,000 & the attack was pushed forward as far as the BROWN LINE.	
"	14th		The Company was under the O.C. for Company Training	

INTELLIGENCE SUMMARY

(Erase heading not required.)

Place	Date	Hour	Summary of Events and Information	Remarks and references to Appendices
RAINCHEVAL N⁵ 10.4			Divisional General presented ribbons to recipients of the M.C. & D.S.O. 2/Lt Gordon & the O.R.s proceeded to Machine Gun Course at CAMIERS.	
"	16th		About 2 p.m. the 99th Inf. Bde ordered the 99th Machine Gun Company to proceed at once to meet Buses in MAILLY VILLAGE. The Company Transpre paraded at 2.30 p.m. & Marched off at 2.30 p.m. for MAILLY, the route was:- REF MAP 57C 1/40,000 - ARQUÈVES, LEALVILLERS, ACHEUX, FORCEVILLE. The following Extract of 99th Inf. Bde Order No.87 received at 8 p.m. to-day stated that the 1st line transport was to be Brigaded at HEDAUVILLE. Brigade Headquarters would close at ARQUÈVES at 2.30 on 17th & reopen at CAFÉ JOURDAIN, MAILLY-MAILLET at same hour. O.C. 99th M.G.Coy would Confer with O.C. 190th M.G.Coy this evening & would take over the line to-morrow morning as at present held by the 190th Inf. Bde.	
MAILLY	17th		Four guns under Lt. Lindsay & 4 guns under 2/Lt Havard proceeded at 5.A.M. to the trenches to take over the 8 gun positions of the 190th M.G. Coy	

Place	Date	Hour	Summary of Events and Information	Remarks and references to Appendices
MAILLY	Oct 17th		99th M.G. Coy with the 8 reserve guns remained in billets at MAILLY.	
"	18th		Gaps in enemy barbed wire are fired at from S₁ & R₁ & R₂ (Ref Map HEBUTERNE July Ref. 1:10,000)	
"	19th		Lt Bowtran received orders to proceed to 11th Machine Gun Coy.	
"	20th		Sgt Thomas arrives as reinforcement to 99th Machine Gun Coy. Lt Bowtran proceeds to N Machine Gun Coy.	
"	21st		99th Machine Machine Gun Coy received 99th Infantry Bde Order No 88 dated 21.10.16. Ref Maps HEBUTERNE Map 1/10,000 Sheet 57C 1/40,000. The 99th Inf Bdy will be relieved by the 15th & 16th Inf Bdes on the 22-10-16. Guides of 5 M.G. teams of 99th M.G. Coy in left Sect. will meet guns of 6th M.G. Coy at Junction of Chau OH AVENUE & EUSTON MAILLY road at 11 AM. Guides of 3 M.G.S of 99th Machine Gun Coy will meet guns of 5th M.G. Coy	

Place	Date	Hour	Summary of Events and Information	Remarks and references to Appendices
MAILLY	Oct 21st		at Junction of ROMAN ROAD & 6th AVENUE at 2.30 pm to deliver them up to the Right Sub Sector. First Line Transport of Brigade were to remain at BEAUSSART. Brigade H.Q. will close at BEAUSSART at 2.20 pm and open at BERTRANCOURT at the same hour.	OK Reg Smith
BERTRANCOURT	22nd		No's 2 & 3 Sections 99th Machine Gun Coy marched off at 2.30 pm for their new billets at BERTRANCOURT via BEAUSSART. Head Quarters and the remainder of the company left MAILLY VILLAGE at 6 pm for BERTRANCOURT & arrived at 7 pm.	
"	23rd		A Brigade Conference was held to-day at 3 pm. O.C. 99th Machine Gun Company attended.	
"	24th		Nothing to Report.	

Place	Date	Hour	Summary of Events and Information	Remarks and references to Appendices
BERTRANCOURT	25th		Nothing to Report.	
"	26th			
"	27			
"	28			
"	29		Following extract from order No 90 received from 99th Inf Bde. dated 29.10.16. stated:- Ref Maps. HEBUTERNE 1/10000. Sheet 57c 1/40,000. 99th Inf Bde will relieve 5th and 6th Bdes in the line to-morrow 30.10.16. The 99th Machine Gun Company will relieve 5th & 6th Brigade Guns under arrangements to be made between O.C's concerned. All movements N E of MAILLY MAILLET will be in Small parties 200 yards interval. 1st Line Transport will not move. Brigade H.Q. will close at BERTRANCOURT at 3pm and reopen at BEAUSSART at the same hour.	
MAILLY	30th		10 Gun Teams under the Coxswain left their billets at 9 A.M. and proceeded to take over the 10 Guns at present held by the 5th & 6th Machine Gun Coy's.	

INTELLIGENCE SUMMARY

(Erase heading not required.)

Place	Date	Hour	Summary of Events and Information	Remarks and references to Appendices
MAILLY	OCT 30		The Head Quarters and remainder of the Company paraded at 10.15 A.M. & proceeded to MAILLY arriving there at 11.20 A.M. when they billeted.	At Bay line off
"	31st		All quiet. 1 ot casualty.	

99th Brigade.
2nd Division.

99th MACHINE GUN COMPANY

NOVEMBER 1 9 1 6

Army Form C. 2118.

WAR DIARY
INTELLIGENCE SUMMARY

(Erase heading not required.)

GHQ. M.G. Co.

Vol 1

Original War Diary

for

November 1916

Place	Date	Hour	Summary of Events and Information	Remarks and references to Appendices

Instructions regarding War Diaries and Intelligence Summaries are contained in F. S. Regs., Part II. and the Staff Manual respectively. Title Pages will be prepared in manuscript.

Army Form C. 2118.

WAR DIARY or INTELLIGENCE SUMMARY
(Erase heading not required.)

Place	Date	Hour	Summary of Events and Information	Remarks and references to Appendices
MAILLY-MAILLETTE	November 1st		The Company moved up to MAILLY from BERTRANCOURT on October 30th and to-day there are 10 guns in the line and 6 guns in reserve at MAILLY. Head quarters are at the Post office. Position of guns in the line :- Ref. MAP. HEBUTERNE TRENCH MAP 1/10000. Mr CHAMPION commanded 4 Guns in reserve line (1) K.33.c.9.8. (2) K.33.d.3.9. (3) K.33.b.9.2. (4) K.33.b.7.5. Mr COURSELL Commanded four guns in support line (1) K.34.d.4.5. (2) K.34.b.0.2. (3) K.34.b.4.4. (4) K.34.b.6.8. Mr THOMAS commanded 2 guns in the front line (1) Q.4.b.4.6. (2) Q.4.b.7.6.	ak. Day. Revort
	2nd		Nothing to report. Trenches in a shocking condition.	
	3rd		" " " Firing took place daily on BEAUMONT HAMEL from R1 Position	
	4th		" " "	
	5th		" " " Gaps in enemy wire were kept open by continual bursts throughout the night from S1, S2, S3, S4, F1 & F2 Positions	
	6th		" " "	

Place	Date	Hour	Summary of Events and Information	Remarks and references to Appendices
MAILLY	Nov 7th		2/Lt THOMAS and his two Gun Teams in F₁ & F₂ positions were relieved by 2/Lt GORDON and the first teams from the Reserve in MAILLY village.	
	Nov 8th		To-day the 99th Machine Gun Coy were relieved in the line by teams from the 5th & 6th Machine Gun Corps. Five guns teams from the Fifth brigade met guides from F₁ F₂ S₁ R₁ R₂ at Coy HQ at 7.15 A.M., while 5 Gun Teams from the 6th Brigade met gun guides from S₂ S₃ S₄ R₃ R₄ positions at Coy HQ at 7.30 A.M. The relief was completed by 12 noon. The company were ordered to remain at MAILLY in reserve.	
	Nov 9th		NOTHING to report.	
	Nov 10th		"Z" day for the attack was commenced to-day. To-day being "W" day.	
	Nov 11th		Nothing to report "X" day.	

Army Form C. 2118.

WAR DIARY or INTELLIGENCE SUMMARY
(Erase heading not required.)

Place	Date	Hour	Summary of Events and Information	Remarks and references to Appendices
Nov 12th MAILLY	12th		"Y" day. The Company paraded in complete fighting order at 10.0 AM for inspection by the Commanding Officer. Red patches were worn on the front of the haversack + blue + yellow distinguishing were worn by every man on his right shoulder. At 11.30 AM. 2 gun teams of No2 Section under Lt Cromwell proceeded up to the trenches with the 1st Royal Berkshires. To-night between 10pm + 3pm the following movements of Section took place:— No1 Section under Lt LINDSAY attached itself to the 22nd Royal Fusiliers + proceeded up to the line. 1 Sub-Section of No2 Section attached itself to the 1st KRRC under Lt GORDON; No3 Section under Lt HAYWARD was attached to the 23rd Royal Fusiliers; No4 Section under Lt CHAMPION remained in reserve with Coy H.Q. and moved up behind the 23rd RF's and was clear of EUSTON MAILLY ½ hour before ZERO	A.M. Day-Lewis(?)
	13th			

Place	Date	Hour	Summary of Events and Information	Remarks and references to Appendices
VIEW TRENCH	13th to 17th		Ref. Maps REDAN {3/5000, PENDANT COPSE 1/10,000} HEBUTERNE	Capt. Day Lewis Pt

It is impossible to give a daily summary of events so I am about to describe the doings of the Sections from the 13th to 17th inclusive.

No. 1. SECTION. At Zero} No 1 Section moved with 22nd Royal Fusiliers 13th} into TOURNAI TRENCH, one sub-section being attached to B Coy and the other sub-section to "D" Coy. In the afternoon of "Z" day this Battalion was ordered to form a defensive flank from the GREEN LINE to our old FRONT LINE. The Battalion was unable to occupy the flank intended but took up a line from K.35.c.38. thence to K.35.a.b.o. and from him to the GREEN LINE at K.35.d.17. The four guns of this section and one Gun of the 6th Brigade, under Lt. Lindsay took up the following positions for —

Army Form C. 2118.

WAR DIARY or INTELLIGENCE SUMMARY

(Erase heading not required.)

Place	Date	Hour	Summary of Events and Information	Remarks and references to Appendices
VIEW TRENCH	Nov. 13th to 17th Cont.		The defence of the Flank at about 6 pm as follows:- The gun of the 6th M.G. Coy remained in reserve with the Left Coy H.Q. at K.35.c.6.6. One gun at K.35.c.35.85 covering the left flank and firing along the southern & western face of the QUADRILATERAL. One gun at K.35.c.4.7. firing from about the junction of BOW STREET and the old GERMAN FRONT LINE to about K.35.h. central. One gun at K.35.c.7.6. firing in N.E. direction to K.35.b. central, and One gun at K.35.c.6.6. firing from K.35.b. central to about K.36.d.6.6. EAST of the GREEN LINE. The 2 Guns of No 2 Section under Lt Cornwall attached to the 1st Royal Berkshires were situated in STIRLING TRENCH at ZERO on 2" clay. at 6.15 AM on the 14th they moved forward with the 1st ROYAL BERKSHIRES. in the attack on MUNICH TRENCH	A.K. Day. Lieut Lt

Army Form C. 2118.

WAR DIARY
or
INTELLIGENCE SUMMARY
(Erase heading not required.)

Instructions regarding War Diaries and Intelligence Summaries are contained in F. S. Regs., Part II. and the Staff Manual respectively. Title Pages will be prepared in manuscript.

Place	Date	Hour	Summary of Events and Information	Remarks and references to Appendices
VIEW TRENCH	Nov 13th 16	TRENCH	Positions for these guns were chosen in SERRE TRENCH near the junction of LAGER ALLEY to protect the Northern flanks of the 1st Royal BERKSHIRES. These two guns remained in their positions until relieved by two teams of the 14th M.G. Coy. It was only found necessary on a very few occasions to bring the guns into action. In one case a belt was fired at a GERMAN party about K 35 trenthail. This party was dispersed. The whole of the defensive flank formed by the 22nd Royal Fusiliers and 1st Royal Berkshires was well covered by the 6 Guns attached to them; very little information can be obtained on to the part taken by No 3 Section and a sub-section of No 2 Section. 2 Guns of No 2 Section under Lt Gordon (wounded) was attached to the 1st K.R.R.C. These two guns were attached to A & D Coys respectively.	a.k. to Sgt. Pruitt

Contd.

2449 Wt. W14957/M90 750,000 1/16 J.B.C. & A. Forms/C.2118/12.

Army Form C. 2118.

WAR DIARY
or
INTELLIGENCE SUMMARY
(Erase heading not required.)

Place	Date	Hour	Summary of Events and Information	Remarks and references to Appendices
VIEW TRENCH	Nov 13th to 17th CONTD.	respectively.	At about 6.15 A.M. on the 14th three Lewis gun teams advanced with the second wave of the 1st K.R.R.C. One gun remained in the old German front line with "D" Coy. and consolidated. About 12 noon on the 14th this team lost touch with D Coy. and after endeavouring to discover their position, moved to the German 2nd line where they were informed that the Battalion was and were unable to find them. This team moved too far south and came into the 51st Divisional area and attached itself to the Argyll & Sutherlands. The team reported at Maitly on the morning of the 17th. The team with "A" Coy. moved forward with it to the GREEN LINE, and took up a position EAST of it in a shell hole. This gun was hit by a shell killing the two men with it. The post taken by No 3 Section attached to the 23rd Royal Fusiliers is very uncertain, as the officer in charge of this section (2Lt Howard) was himself after being wounded. The Section Sergeant was also	A.K. & 2y-Lewis Lt

Place	Date	Hour	Summary of Events and Information	Remarks and references to Appendices
VIEW TRENCH	Nov 13th to 17th Cont'd	—also.	wounded early in the operations. This section lost 14 men out of the total casualties of 26. One Gun and its team was completely knocked out. Two men & the gun only of No 2 team reported to HQ of the Company at VIEW TRENCH at 1pm on the 14th. These men had lost their guns. This team was replaced by one team from the reserve section & was sent to the H.Q. 23rd R.F's at WHITE CITY, who were then in support. No 4 Section moved into VIEW TRENCH at 12 ZERO 13th and remains in reserve. The Gun Team sent to the 28th R.F's was replaced by another team from 6 reserve men in MAILLY. On the morning of the 16th, 1 Sub-section of reserve section was attached to the 1st K.R.R.C. and the other to the 23rd R.F's at VALLADE & ELLIS SQUARE respectively in replace than of No 3 & No 2 Sections They being in reserve to the 14th Brigade.	O.K. Sgt. Hewitt

Army Form C. 2118.

WAR DIARY
or
INTELLIGENCE SUMMARY
(Erase heading not required.)

Instructions regarding War Diaries and Intelligence Summaries are contained in F. S. Regs., Part II. and the Staff Manual respectively. Title Pages will be prepared in manuscript.

Place	Date	Hour	Summary of Events and Information	Remarks and references to Appendices
VIEW TRENCH	NOV 13th 16 17th Contd.		Brigade. These two Subsections moved back to MAILLY at 3pm on 17th when their Battalion were relieved. No 1 & 2 Sections were to have been relieved by teams of the 14th A/14 G. Coy on the night of the 16/16th, But this company did not arrive till 6 AM on the morning of the 16th. The relief of the Six guns then in the line was arranged for 8pm on the night of the 16/17th. No 1 Section completed their relief by 3.0 AM on the 17th and returned to MAILLY. The Sub-Section of No 2 Section was not to be relieved till the night of the 17/18 owing to an error caused by the two teams of the 14th 14th M.G. Coy. moving off before the two guides had arrived. This Sub-section was relieved by 3.30 am on the 18th.	A.K. day. hearst

Army Form C. 2118.

WAR DIARY
or
INTELLIGENCE SUMMARY
(Erase heading not required.)

Instructions regarding War Diaries and Intelligence Summaries are contained in F. S. Regs., Part II. and the Staff Manual respectively. Title Pages will be prepared in manuscript.

Place	Date	Hour	Summary of Events and Information	Remarks and references to Appendices
SARTON	17th	8pm	ATO The Company less No 4 Section, HQ's + one Sub section of No 2 Section proceeded to SARTON (REF MAP LENS 1/100,000) in Motor Lorries arriving at 6 p.m. Lt. Day-Lewis commanded this Party; the Transport remained at BEAUSSART.	A.K. Day-Lewis
TERRA-MESNIL	18		Lt. Day-Lewis received orders this morning to march his party to TERRA MESNIL + to clear of SARTON by 10.A.M. The party arrived here at 11 A.M., and about 1 hour afterwards were met by Capt Snell and the remainder of the Company. The Transport arrived from BEAUSSART at 2 p.m.	
BEAUVAL	19-		REF MAP LENS (II) 1/100,000. Orders were received this morning to march to BEAUVAL. The Company were to pass ROAD JUNCTION NW Corner of TERRA MESNIL at 2.30 p.m.	

2449 Wt. W14957/M90 750,000 1/16 J.B.C. & A. Forms/C.2118/12.

Army Form C. 2118.

WAR DIARY or INTELLIGENCE SUMMARY

(Erase heading not required.)

Instructions regarding War Diaries and Intelligence Summaries are contained in F. S. Regs., Part II and the Staff Manual respectively. Title Pages will be prepared in manuscript.

Place	Date	Hour	Summary of Events and Information	Remarks and references to Appendices
BEAUVAL	19th	2.30 pm	The Company arrived in billets at 4.30 pm.	C.K. Day. Lewis Lt
BEAUVAL	20th		The Company was formed up in the Main Street at 3.30 pm as General Sir Douglas HAIG passed through the village.	
BERNEUIL	21st		Orders were received for us to proceed to BERNEUIL to-day. REF MAP LENS (II)/10000 Starting Point was the X.Rds 1/8" S.E. of CANDAS Station and the machine gun Company were to pass it at 10.5 A.M. Previous billets were to be quitted at 8.5 A.M. The Company arrived in their new billets at 10 pm.	
BERNEUIL	22nd		Remained in same billets — nothing to report.	
MESNIL DONQUEUR	23rd		The Company received orders to moved to MESNIL DONQUEUR & were to clear of BERNEUIL by 10.30 A.M. they The Company arrived in billets at 2 pm.	

Army Form C. 2118.

WAR DIARY
or
INTELLIGENCE SUMMARY
(Erase heading not required.)

Instructions regarding War Diaries and Intelligence Summaries are contained in F.S. Regs., Part II. and the Staff Manual respectively. Title Pages will be prepared in manuscript.

Place	Date	Hour	Summary of Events and Information	Remarks and references to Appendices
ARGENVILLERS	24th		The Company received orders to move to ARGENVILLERS (Ref Map MINUS (II)/100000) The route was to be via MAISON ROLLAND - COULON VILLERS - ST RIQUIER. Head of the company was to pass DOMQUEUR - YVRENCH ROAD at 11.45 AM. The Company arrived in their new billets at 2 pm.	ABBEVILLE 1/100000 A/R. Day. Lewis H
DRUCAT	25th		The Company was ordered to move to-day to DRUCAT (Ref Map 1/100000). Route was to be through MILLENCOURT - CAOURS. Starting point on ROAD JUNCTION IMMEDIATELY S of ARGENVILLERS was to be passed at 10 AM. The Company in billets at 11.45 AM. WEATHER VERY WET.	ABBEVILLE 1/100000
DRUCAT	26th		NOTHING to Report. 2/Lt CHAMPION + 20 O.R's left for course at CAHIERES. Lt LINDSAY proceeded on leave to ENGLAND. 2/Lts WATSON + MILLER join the Company any from leave.	

Army Form C. 2118.

WAR DIARY
or
INTELLIGENCE SUMMARY
(Erase heading not required.)

Place	Date	Hour	Summary of Events and Information	Remarks and references to Appendices
HANCHY	Nov 27th		The Company were ordered to move to-day to YVRENCH. Rt Maps. ABBEVILLE 1/100,000. Route was the X ROADS immediately N of DRUCAT-LENS. MILLENCOURT - ST RIQUIER - ONEUX. Starting point was X Roads Junct. immediately East of MILLENCOURT & the company was to pass it at 10.0 A.M. The Company arrived in billets at 2.30 pm. The orders received were that we went to billet at YVRENCH, as there was no room in the village the company moved to HANCHY. Lt RICHARDS joins the company from BASE.	A.K. Way. Lewis Lt.
HANCHY	28th		Nothing to report	
"	29th		" " "	
"	30th		" " "	app. O.K. Day. Lewis Lt.

99th Brigade.
2nd Division.

99th MACHINE GUN COMPANY

DECEMBER 1 9 1 6

INTELLIGENCE SUMMARY

(Erase heading not required.)

99th M.G. Co

No. 9

Place	Date	Hour	Summary of Events and Information	Remarks and references to Appendices
HANCHY	Dec 1st to 31st		The Company remains in present billets & carries out daily training.	A.F. Day. Lieut ff

A.F. Day. Lieut ff

2ND DIVISION
99TH INFY BDE

99TH MACHINE GUN COY.

JAN-DEC 1917.

Box 1323

99th Brigade / 2nd Division.

99th MACHINE GUN COMPANY ::: JANUARY 1917.

Army Form C. 2118

WAR DIARY
or
INTELLIGENCE SUMMARY
(Erase heading not required.)

99th L.T.M.B.C

Vol 10

Off. Day. Lawill

Place	Date	Hour	Summary of Events and Information	Remarks and references to Appendices
HANCHY	JAN 1ST		Training Continued in rear billets.	
"	2ND		Capt HOLLIDAY arrived to-day to take over command of the company.	
"	3rd 4th		} Training Continued.	
"	5th		A brigade attack exercise was carried out this morning on the ground about A11-12 & A17+18 a+b. The wood at A15 b.12. represented Pys & this latter village was the objective of the Division. Ref Map. ST RIQUEUR 1/20,000.	
"	6th		A divisional attack exercise was carried out this afternoon on the	

Place	Date	Hour	Summary of Events and Information	Remarks and references to Appendices
HANCHY	JAN 6th	Cont.	Same ground as the Brigade Scheme yesterday. The 22nd & 23rd RF's were the attacking force, the former on the right & the latter on the left, of our brigade frontage. The Berkshires were in support & the 1st KRRC were the Mopping up Battalion. The 99th Machine Gun Coy was distributed as follows:- 4 Guns were allotted to the 22nd RF's, 4 Guns to the 23rd RF's, 4 Guns to the 1st R. Berkshires & four were kept in reserve at company Headquarters on DYKE ROAD about A.H.C.1.2. Lt A.W. Day-Lewis & 1 O.R. proceeded on leave to ENGLAND to-day.	H Davy Maj CR 2nd

Army Form C. 2118

WAR DIARY
INTELLIGENCE SUMMARY

Place	Date	Hour	Summary of Events and Information	Remarks and references to Appendices
HANCHY	Jan 7th		Day Quiet & Coy training in vicinity of billets.	
"	8th	2.0 pm	To-day the Company was inspected by the commanding officer. The following orders were received from 99th Inf Bde. Ref Map LENS SHEET 11 1/100,000. (a) The 99th Machine Gun Coy were to move to ABBEVILLE on 14/1/100,000. to the BERNAVILLE AREA on JAN 9th. (b) On JAN 11th it would march to MARIEUX AREA. (c) On 12th & 13th Jan. the 2nd Division would move up & take over line now held by 51st Division. 1st line transport would accompany their units.	
DOMESNONT	Jan 9th		The Company arrived here at 6.30 pm after having marched from HANCHY. The Company paraded at 11.30 AM this morning and	

WAR DIARY or INTELLIGENCE SUMMARY

Army Form C. 2118

Place	Date	Hour	Summary of Events and Information	Remarks and references to Appendices
DOMESMONT	JAN 9th	Contd.	REF MAPS LENS 11 1/100,000 ABBEVILLE 19 1/100,000 Passed the Brigade Starting point X RDS. ¼ MILE N of M in MASURES at 1.10 p.m. The route taken was HANCHY, HIN DE CRAMONT, CROSS ROADS and LONGVILLERS. The distance covered was 9¼ miles.	
"	JAN 10th		Rested on DOMESMONT.	
TERRA-MESNIL	JAN 11th		Orders were received yesterday for the Company to proceed to TERRA MESNIL. 99th Inf Bde Order No 105 10.1.17 was as follows:— 99th Inf Bde Groups will march to the MARIEUX AREA. REF LENS 11 1/100,000. The March table for 99th Machine Gun Coy was as follows:— from DOMESMONT — TERRA MESNIL. STARTING POINT fork road cutting C in CANDAS. Time of passing starting point 1.35 p.m. Route BERNAVILLE — FEINVILLERS — thence CANDAS XROADS immediately S of 2nd U in ANCIEN MIN DE VALHEUREUX — BEAUVAL thence by Road which follows the railway to BEAUQUESNE. The Company arrived in their new billets at 6.30 p.m.	

WAR DIARY
INTELLIGENCE SUMMARY.

Army Form C. 211

Place	Date	Hour	Summary of Events and Information	Remarks and references to Appendices
TERRA-MESNIL	Jan 12th		Company route here to-day.	Army Form X.?
" BUZINCOURT	Jan 13th		Company were ordered to move from TERRA-MESNIL to BUZINCOURT to-day. They arrived in their new billets at 6.0 p.m.	
BUZINCOURT	Jan 14th		Company rested. 2/Lt. S. MULLER and 5 ors. left Coy for Course on Camera.	

Army Form C. 2118.

WAR DIARY
or
INTELLIGENCE SUMMARY.
(Erase heading not required.)

Place	Date	Hour	Summary of Events and Information	Remarks and references to Appendices
BOUZINCOURT	JAN 15th		Company trained.	
"	16th		The Commanding Officer & Lt LINDSAY reconnoitred ground in the vicinity of AVELUY and OVILLERS.	
"	17th		The Brigadier inspected the Companies billets. Snowfall throughout the day. 2 OR's proceeded on leave.	
"	18th		Commanding Officer & Section Officers did a reconnaissance of the ground around AVELUY & OVILLERS.	
"	19th		Lt A.K. DAY, LEWIS was returned from leave. Commanding Officer & Lt Connell went out on Staff ride	

Army Form C. 2118.

WAR DIARY
or
~~INTELLIGENCE SUMMARY~~

(Erase heading not required.)

Instructions regarding War Diaries and Intelligence Summaries are contained in F. S. Regs., Part II. and the Staff Manual respectively. Title pages will be prepared in manuscript.

Place	Date	Hour	Summary of Events and Information	Remarks and references to Appendices
AVELUY	Jan. 20th		The 99th Machine Gun Coy were ordered to relieve the 6th Inf Bde in the Support area to-day. The Company moved off from BUZINCOURT by sections at two minute interval and arrived in their new billets at AVELUY at 6.30 pm	All Recy - Letters 11
"	21st		Company improved billets	
"	22nd		Found working party by night 75 men — by day 10 men	
"	23		" "	
"	24		C.O. & 2nd I/C visited 6th M.G.Coy in line	
"	25		Working parties as above.	
"	26		Brigade Conference & Corps Conference. 9th Infantry & Cavalry went round guns in line.	
"	27		Working parties as above	

WAR DIARY or INTELLIGENCE SUMMARY

Army Form C. 2118.

Place	Date	Hour	Summary of Events and Information	Remarks and references to Appendices
R.29 Central	28th		Ref. Map 57C. S.E. 1/20,000. The Company relieved the 6th M.G. Coy in the line b. day. 2nd Lieut LINDSAY with 4 GUN TEAMS relieved the 4 guns in the right Sector — R₁, R₂, S₁, R₆ Lt Cansell " " " " left " — R₄, R₅, S₂, R₃ 2/Lt Thomas " " " " centre " — O₁, O₂, O₃, O₄ Headquarters were situated at R.29 Central. The Transport remained in huts at AVELUY.	
"	29		Nothing to report.	
"	30		O guns fired on tracks defence tracks line.	
"	31		O & R guns kept up casual fire on tracks & cross roads in trenches. O.K. Day. Rain. 2nd Lt R Bennett Parker & 2nd Lt Cantly 4.4.18	

99th Brigade / 2nd Division.

99th MACHINE GUN COMPANY ::: FEBRUARY 1917.

WAR DIARY
or
INTELLIGENCE SUMMARY.

(Erase heading not required.)

Army Form C. 2118

99th Machine Gun Coy

Vol XI

WAR DIARY
or
INTELLIGENCE SUMMARY

(Erase heading not required.)

Army Form C. 2118.

Place	Date	Hour	Summary of Events and Information	Remarks and references to Appendices
	FEB. 1st		Ref. Map 57 C. S.E. 1/20,000. Company H.Q. at R 29 Central. The half Company in the line was relieved today by the Section at Wallace Cranville Huts. Lt. Richards with 4 gun teams took over the Rt. Sect. R1,R2,S,R6. Lt. Champion " " " " Lt. Sect. R4,R5,R3. 2/Lt Watson " " " Centre Sect. O1,O2,O3,O4. The Half Coy. relieved, returned to Wallace Cranville Huts. Guns and tripods at R3 was put out of action by shrapnel. Casualties 1 O.R. killed. 1 O.R. wounded.	R Crabbe Lt
	2.		Nothing to report. C.O. proceeded on leave.	
	3.			
	4.			

Army Form C. 2118.

WAR DIARY
or
INTELLIGENCE SUMMARY
(Erase heading not required.)

Instructions regarding War Diaries and Intelligence Summaries are contained in F. S. Regs., Part II. and the Staff Manual respectively. Title Pages will be prepared in manuscript.

Place	Date	Hour	Summary of Events and Information	Remarks and references to Appendices
BOUZINCOURT	5th		The Company was relieved in the Line by the 5th M.G. Co, and moved to BOUZINCOURT.	R. Castle
	6th		The Transport remains at Cromwell Huts.	
	7th		The Company cleaned guns and equipment.	
	8th		Company training. Route march.	
	9th		C.O. recalled from leave. Arrived to-day.	
	10th		The Company was inspected by the Commanding Officer.	
	11th		Company training.	
			Company rested. Lt Richards, Lt Wall & 2/Lt Thomas went into line to visit 5th M.G.Co. guns.	
	12th		A Brigade attack exercise was carried out on ground N.E. of BOUZINCOURT. (Ref. map [57.D.S.E.] W.1.2.7.8. in which the whole Company took part.	

2449 Wt. W14957/M90 750,000 1/16 J.B.C. & A. Forms/C.2118/12.

WAR DIARY
INTELLIGENCE SUMMARY

Army Form C. 2118.

Place	Date	Hour	Summary of Events and Information	Remarks and references to Appendices
BOUZINCOURT.	13th to 14th		Brigade attack exercise again carried out on same ground. Only officers & N.Cos of M.G.C. present. Company training.	Plate 11
	15th		The Company paraded in complete fighting order at 10.0 A.M. for inspection by the Commanding Officer. At 4 p.m. the sections moved off to join the Battalions they were attached to, which were as follows:—	
			3 guns under Lt. Lindsay attd. to 22nd Royal Fusiliers.	
			3 " " 2Lt Watson — " 22nd R.F.	
			4 " " [Lt. Champion] " 23rd R.F.	
			[2Lt Thomas]	
			3 " " Lt. Richards " K.R.R.	
			3 " " Lt. Counsell under O.C. 99 M.G.Co.	

Army Form C./2118.

WAR DIARY
or
INTELLIGENCE SUMMARY.

(Erase heading not required.)

Instructions regarding War Diaries and Intelligence Summaries are contained in F. S. Regs., Part II. and the Staff Manual respectively. Title pages will be prepared in manuscript.

Place	Date	Hour	Summary of Events and Information	Remarks and references to Appendices
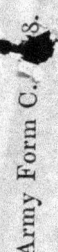	15th.		H.Q. removed to Cranwell Huts and the 3 gun teams under Lt. Cranwell were billeted at Wallace Huts close by.	Renault.
	16th.		"Y" Day. The C.O. visited the Sections under their respective units at Wolf Huts & Ovillers Huts. At 9-0. P.M. H.Q. and Lt. Cranwell's gun teams went up into the Line.	
	17th.		"Z" Day. "Zero" was at 5.45 A.M. The attack started in total darkness but good direction was kept and the first objective taken. Lt. Cranwell in charge of support guns was wounded before the "Zero hour". After advancing beyond the first objective direction was to some extent lost and owing to casualties the gun teams in some cases became disorganised for	

WAR DIARY
or
INTELLIGENCE SUMMARY.

(Erase heading not required.)

Place	Date	Hour	Summary of Events and Information	Remarks and references to Appendices
	17th		a short time. Lt. Champion & 2/Lt. Thomas were both went put out of action and it was afterwards found that 2/Lt. Thomas had been killed. Lt. Richards was also wounded in this neighbourhood. As there was an absence of guns on the extreme right of the first objective Lt. Day-Lewis went up with 2 support guns and made good his position there. At the end of operations the disposition of guns was as follows. On the left, 2 guns under 2/Lt Watson. In the centre, 2 of Lt. Champion's guns under Sergt. McLoughlin. On the right, 2 guns under Lt Day Lewis, one of which defended a patrol of the flank. On the right flank 1 gun under Sergt. Vaughan, and 3 guns under Lt. Lindsay. Total Casualties. 1 officer killed. 3 officers wounded and 32 O.R.S.	R Scott.

WAR DIARY
or
INTELLIGENCE SUMMARY.
(Erase heading not required.)

Army Form C. 2118.

Instructions regarding War Diaries and Intelligence Summaries are contained in F. S. Regs., Part II. and the Staff Manual respectively. Title pages will be prepared in manuscript.

Place	Date	Hour	Summary of Events and Information	Remarks and references to Appendices
	18th & 19th		The Company was relieved on the night of 18th–19th by the 6th M.G.Co. The last team came out about 6.0.A.M. The Company were in billets at Vena Hill in fragments. (Ref Map. 57 b S.E.) x 24 Central. Transport remains at Cromwell Huts.	J.C.Newell Lt
	20th		Cleaning guns & equipment. Two Stokes teams under 2/Lt Miller were sent to the arial the Anti aircraft guns in the neighbourhood of La Brioelle.	
	21st		A working party of 50 men was sent up to P. Dump at 6.30 p.m. & a similar party as the one last night to La Brioelle.	
	22nd		Working party and anti-aircraft party as before. 2/Lts Blackburne, Lunn, & Ackland arrived as reinforcements.	
	23rd		The same parties sent out as before. 2/Lts Clausen & Bundy arrived as reinforcements.	

Army Form C. 2118.

WAR DIARY
or
INTELLIGENCE SUMMARY.

(Erase heading not required.)

Place	Date	Hour	Summary of Events and Information	Remarks and references to Appendices
USNA HILL	24th		Company training.	
	25th		Anti-aircraft party as before.	
	26th		Working party & anti-aircraft parties as before. Same parties sent out.	Coy notes.
	27th		Company training.	
	28th		Pack saddlery Inspection by Brig. General. 30 animals.	

99th Brigade / 2nd Division.

99th MACHINE GUN COMPANY ::: MARCH 1917.

Army Form C. 2118.

WAR DIARY
INTELLIGENCE SUMMARY.
(Erase heading not required.)

99th M.G.Co.

Vol 12

March 1917

WAR DIARY or INTELLIGENCE SUMMARY

Army Form C. 2118.

Place	Date	Hour	Summary of Events and Information	Remarks and references to Appendices
MARCH USNA HILL	1st		Company remained in same billets and continued training.	
"	2nd		Continued training; received Bde Order 115 to the effect that this company would relieve the 5th Machine Gun Coy on the night 8/9 March.	
"	3rd		57DSE 1/30000 The Company quitted present billets at 2.15 p.m. and marched to the Quarry on the BAPAUME ROAD. No 1 Section remained at H.Q. at R29 central while 6 guns under 2/Lt ACKLAND & 2/Lt BUNDY proceeded to GRUNDY TRENCH; 2 guns under 2/Lt STRETTELL. MILLER and 2/Lt BACKHOUSE proceeded to BELOW TRENCH. No 3 Section under 2/Lt WATSON remained in reserve at H.Q.	

WAR DIARY or INTELLIGENCE SUMMARY

Army Form C. 2118.

Place	Date	Hour	Summary of Events and Information	Remarks and references to Appendices
67D9E Please R.29 AnKel	3rd		Relief Completed was reported by 8.30 p.m. About 11.0 p.m. 2/Lt CLAUSEN with 4 Guns belonging to No 1 Section proceeded to take up positions in GALLWITZ Trench. He was reported in position at 3.0 AM	2/Lt Bay Lewis
	4th		NOTHING TO REPORT.	
	5th		2/Lt LUNN proceeded to join 2/Lt CLAUSEN. 2/Lt BUNDEY & 2/Lt BACKHOUSE interchanged their location.	
	6th		NOTHING TO REPORT. Wire being kept open by bursts of fire.	
	7th		ditto	
	8th		Headquarters & reserve section moved up to BELOW TRENCH	
	9th		The 1st KRRC & 1st ROYAL BERKSHIRES attached GREVILLERS	
	10th		which at 6.0 AM — the Company 2 3rd RF's was attached to 1st KRRC.	

WAR DIARY
INTELLIGENCE SUMMARY

Army Form C. 2118.

Place	Date	Hour	Summary of Events and Information	Remarks and references to Appendices
BELOW TRENCH	10th	5.70SE 1/20,000	The 99th Machine Gun Coy cooperated with the above Battalions by putting over a barrage in conjunction with the artillery. 8 guns of the barrage 12 guns of the 99th Coy together with 6 guns of the 6th opened fire at the same time as the artillery barrage & three hundred yards behind it. This barrage lifted with the artillery until reaching LOUPART TRENCH when a steady fire was kept up. Bursts of fire were kept up the following day until the Company was relieved by the 5th M.G.Coy about 8.0 p.m.	
ALBERT	11th		Company rests in billets	
	12th		" " " trained	
	13th		" " " "	
	14th		" " " "	
USNA HILL	15th		The Company moved to USNA HILL this afternoon at 2.15pm.	

Army Form C. 2118.

WAR DIARY
or
INTELLIGENCE SUMMARY
(Erase heading not required.)

Remarks and references to Appendices: Oct Rec II —

Place	Date	Hour	Summary of Events and Information
USNA HILL	16th		Company carried on with training.
	17th		" "
	18th		" "
	19th		The Company moved to huts in ALBERT.
ALBERT.	20		⎫
	21		⎬ Company carried out training programme.
	22		⎪
	23		⎪
	24		⎭
CONTAY	25		REF. MAP 1/100,000. The Company received orders N°171 of 99(?) of 8.08 to move to CONTAY. The Coy marched off at 11.20 am arrived in huts at CONTAY at 2.45 pm

Army Form C. 2118.

WAR DIARY
or
INTELLIGENCE SUMMARY.
(Erase heading not required.)

Instructions regarding War Diaries and Intelligence Summaries are contained in F. S. Regs., Part II. and the Staff Manual respectively. Title pages will be prepared in manuscript.

Place	Date	Hour	Summary of Events and Information	Remarks and references to Appendices
AMPLIERS	26		RUYNARD LENS 1/100,000. Coy received order w.122. 99th Inf Bde to move to AMPLIERS. The Coy marched off at 10.0 AM & arrived in new billets at 2.40 pm.	
BONNIERES	27		The Company received order no 123 of 99th Inf Bde to move to new billets at BONNIERES. The Company paraded at 10.0 AM and arrived in new billets at 3.55 pm.	
BLANGERS-MONT	28		Order No 124 99th Inf Bde ordered the 99th M.G. Coy to proceed to billets at BLANGERSMONT. The Company paraded at 10.15 AM & arrived in new billets at 3.40 pm.	
"	29		Company made entrenchment reccie.	
"	30		The Company received Order No 126 99th Inf BM to move to new billets at SAINS-LEZ-PERNES. They moved off at 9.40 AM & arrived in new billets at 2.50 pm.	
"	31			

99th Brigade / 2nd Division.

99th MACHINE GUN COMPANY:::: APRIL 1917.

99th M.G. Coy

War Diary for April 1917

Army Form C.2118.

WAR DIARY
or
INTELLIGENCE SUMMARY

(Erase heading not required.)

99th Machine Gun Coy

Place	Date	Hour	Summary of Events and Information	Remarks and references to Appendices
SAINS LES PERNES	1917 April 1		2nd Lt FUNN took over Transport duty - 1st Wall to No 2 Section. Training in Billet Area.	
	4/5		O.C. & 2nd i/C reconnoitred line ECURIE - ROCLINCOURT. Surplus Kits to Divisional dump at BRUAY.	
	6		Good Friday. Voluntary Church Service.	
	7	12.30 PM	Marched to DIEVAL - arrived 3.30 PM	
	8		Sunday.	
	9	9 AM	Training.	
	10	9.30 AM 4.30 PM	Marched to Y HUTS. ARRAS - ST. POL ROAD. (SNOWSTORM.) C.O. & Lt Hoall proceeded with G.O.C. to ROCLINCOURT to arrange relief for following day with 152 M.G. Company failing has him.	
Arret C.60	11	9 AM	C.O. & Hoall proceeded and arranged relief with 152 M.G. Company. Company arrived at H.Q. at A24a 6.0 Sheet 51 B.N.W. Relief Completed at 6.30 AM. The relief was carried out in a heavy Snowstorm.	
	12		Q.M. Stores moved to MAROEUIL along Transport.	
	13		Nothing to report. 1st K.R.R.C. divisional Railway Unit not fully authorised up - 23rd R.F. moving in Conjunction. Lt DAY LEWIS 2nd i/C to Hospital.	
	14		3 Sections moved forward to positions - B21 A87 - B27 A59 /B22 C95. Sheet B28 B1.9 /51B NW	

WAR DIARY
or
INTELLIGENCE SUMMARY

Army Form C.2118

99th M.G. Co

Place	Date	Hour	Summary of Events and Information	Remarks and references to Appendices
A.	April 14		Company H.Q. moved forward to MAISON DELACOTE, about B26 d 5.2. One Section moved at Dusk to position at about B23 c 5.5. to fire on OPPY - TENDIN line and OPPY Road. 4000 rounds fired.	
	15		Some shelling - no casualties.	
			Transport & QM Stores moved to bivouacs at about A28 c 3.9	
	16		Arranged Relief by 190 M.G. Company and 6 M.G. Company.	
	17		190 M.G. Company took over 1 Section which went to reserve leaving 2 Sections on Railway Embankment.	
	18		2 Sections relieved by 6 M.G. Company. Company proceeded to Reserve at about A2 & B7.9	
	19		Cleaning Guns etc.	
	20		Capt A.P. SKEVINGTON arrived to take over Command. 2nd Lt R.J. GRIFFITHS arrived.	

WAR DIARY
or
INTELLIGENCE SUMMARY.

(Erase heading not required.)

Army Form C. 2118.

Instructions regarding War Diaries and Intelligence Summaries are contained in F.S. Regs., Part II. and the Staff Manual respectively. Title pages will be prepared in manuscript.

Place	Date	Hour	Summary of Events and Information	Remarks and references to Appendices
51ᵗ NW A28 b 7.9	21ˢᵗ		Company remained in Roeux and carried on training.	
	22ⁿᵈ		Nothing to report	
	23ʳᵈ		Nothing to report	
	24		Nothing to report	
	25		Company found working parties for repairing roads and making mud tracks	
	26		ditto	
	27.		Company paraded at 7.15 pm to go into the line under 2ⁿᵈ Lᵗ Clever, Bundey, Watson, Stuttelf, Miller, Griffith and Rochfort. Met 93 at 7.30 pm to support an attack by the 5ᵗʰ & 6ᵗʰ Brigades. No casualties.	
	28.		Barrage fire opened at 4.25 AM on roads & tracks in rear of OPPY on both flanks. The new movement in enemy lines on either flank all day. At 8 p.m. a German counter attack developed but was frustrated. Very heavy shelling in retaliation. The Coy support an attack by the 5ᵗʰ & 6ᵗʰ Brigades. Barrage fire was opened at 8·00 pm on ground in rear of OPPY. Very heavy shelling in retaliation.	
	29		A Coy relieved the B & M & C Coy, who were supporting us on the attack on the 29ᵗʰ, then shelling fairly heavy.	
	30.		At 2 a.m. the Huns heavily shelled the front position and graveyard near road gas Headquartery shells. This lasted until 7 a.m. NCOs 1 + 3 mortars relieved by the 92ⁿᵈ Coy and went back to Roeux at A28. b.7.9.	
	May 1.			

99th Brigade / 2nd Division.

99th Brigade MACHINE GUN COMPANY ::: M A Y 1917.

Army Form C. 2118.

WAR DIARY
INTELLIGENCE SUMMARY
(Erase heading not required.)

99th M.G. Coy

Vol 14

Place	Date	Hour	Summary of Events and Information	Remarks and references to Appendices
51B N.W. SHEET II A.28.b.7.9	May 1		At 2 AM the Huns heavily shelled the gun positions & ground in rear with gas shells, making relief of the teams until 9 A.M. Nos 1 & 3 Sections were relieved by the 92nd Coy and trekked to Rivière at A.28.b.7.9.	
	2		Nos 2 & 4 sections still in the line under 2nd Lt Rushmer & 2nd Lt Shadwell with Nos 1 & 3 under 2nd Lieuts _____ & Lt Watson went in took his and relieve the 5" A.F. Coy. They took up position to support the attack	
	3		The Coy supported the attack by the 99th Infantry Brigade. Fire was maintained all day and a steam counter-attack broke through our machine gun barrage fire; Battle casualties during the action were 26/4/17 - 3/5/17 - 8 killed (O.R.) 1 O.R. died of wounds and S.O. Rushmer wounded from 10 billets at A.28.b.9.9. 2nd Lt Simmon joined the Coy.	
			Coy were relieved by 13th M.G. Coy. The Coy moved off at 3.30 pm & marches to X Huts Ecoivres.	
LENS SHEET II	4.		Coy rested at X Huts	
	5.		Coy moved to Gurton and arrived there at 4 P.M.	
	6.		ditto	
	7		Company carried out training in billeting area.	
	8		ditto	
	9		ditto	
	10.		Coy moved to Mont St Eloy and arrived there at 5.45 P.M.	
	11-16		Company carried out Training in billeting area.	

Army Form C. 2118.

WAR DIARY
or
INTELLIGENCE SUMMARY.
(Erase heading not required.)

Place	Date	Hour	Summary of Events and Information	Remarks and references to Appendices
LENS.II.	May 17		Coy moved to billets in Angres and remained there at 11 A.M.	H.Q. at ETRAT des Eclus
	18 19 20 21		Parade under Section Officers in billetting area	
	19 20		Officers paraded at 2 p.m. for tactical exercise	
	22		O.C. and 2 i/c went out the line to arrange taking over. 1 Reinforcement arrived from 5" M.G. Coy	
	23		No 4 Section under 2nd Lt Perry went in to relieve the 95" M.G. Coy; section in the Red Line.	
	24		The Company left billets at 8 p.m. to relieve the 13" M.G. Coy - No 1 & 3 sections in front system. No 2 Section in Reserve.	
	25 to 31		Company in the line.	

Officer i/c Coy

99th Brigade / 2nd Divison.

99th MACHINE GUN COMPANY ::: JUNE 1917.

Army Form C. 2118.

WAR DIARY
or
INTELLIGENCE SUMMARY.
(Erase heading not required.)

WO 15

99th M.G. Coy
Erebus
June 1917

Army Form C. 2118.

WAR DIARY
INTELLIGENCE SUMMARY
(Erase heading not required.)

Instructions regarding War Diaries and Intelligence Summaries are contained in F. S. Regs., Part II. and the Staff Manual respectively. Title Pages will be prepared in manuscript.

Place	Date	Hour	Summary of Events and Information	Remarks and references to Appendices
SHEET. 51B N.W. B.15 central.	1917 1st June		Guns in line on OPPY front. CASUALTIES. 4 O.R. KILLED, 30 O.R. WOUNDED.	
	2nd June		Lt. WATSON proceeded on leave.	
	3rd		Lt. STRETTELL-MILLER proceeded on leave.	
	5th		Lt. V. ST CLARE HILL joined the Company as 2nd in Command.	
	6th		Gas Bombardment of enemy trenches at 1.A.M.	
	13th		Lt. WATSON returned from leave.	
	14th		Coy relieved in the line by the guns of the 13th M.G. Coy. Rendez-vous (Jul. 15th) at Western end, Essex Walk 3.30 A.M.	
	15th	3.30 P.M.	Coy proceeded to new Camp at Bois de MAROUEIL arrived at 6.30 A.M. Lt. STRETTELL-MILLER returned from leave.	
	16th		Coy parades.	
	17th		Church parade.	
	18th		Orders received at 3.30 A.M. to be prepared to move. 2nd Lt. BACKHOUSE proceeded to Bethune as billeting officer.	
	19th		Coy parade.	
BETHUNE COMBINED SHEET.	20th		Transport proceeded to BETHUNE leaving camp at 4 A.M. The Company proceeded to BETHUNE by bus from ECOIVRES. Paraded at 8.30 A.M. Arrived in Billets at 2.15 P.M.	
	21st		Coy paraded at 8.45 A.M. and proceeded to NOYELLES to relieve 204th M.G. Coy and arrived there at 11 A.M. 2 guns under 2nd Lt. STRETTELL-MILLER relieved the 2 guns on the line of 204th M.G. Coy. Remainder of Coy occupied the billets vacated by 204th M.G. Coy. 2nd Lt. GRIFFITH R.J. proceeded on leave. Transport lines at LE QUESNOY.	
	22nd	7 P.M.	Coy received orders to move to Billets at ANNEQUIN. Coy reached new billets at 9.45 P.M.	
	23rd		Lt. WALL R.L. proceeded on leave. Day quiet.	

Army Form C. 2118.

WAR DIARY
or
INTELLIGENCE SUMMARY
(Erase heading not required.)

Instructions regarding War Diaries and Intelligence Summaries are contained in F. S. Regs., Part II. and the Staff Manual respectively. Title Pages will be prepared in manuscript.

Place	Date	Hour	Summary of Events and Information	Remarks and references to Appendices
BETHUNE COURINET SREET.	24th		Quiet day. Cloud forecast.	
	25th		2 Guns in the line fired on German Relief. Lt WATSON o MILLER in charge.	
	26th		CAPT. SKEVINGTON A.P. to A.H.Q as A/A.D.M.G.O. Lt V. St CLARE-HILL in command of the Company. Lt WATSON relieved Lt STRETTELL. MILLER in the line.	
	27th		Auchy bombarded by our artillery; M.G.s co-operated.	
	28th		12 guns get in. Coy relieved the 12 guns in the 1st C.M.G.S. Remaining 2 guns g. N°4 Section relieved the 2 guns of that section already in the line. Officers in the line Lt WATSON, 2nd Lt ACKLAND, 2nd Lt BUNDEY.	
	29th		Day quiet. 2nd Lt BERRY relieved Lt WATSON in the line.	
	30.		ditto. Lt WATSON proceeded to CAMIERS for a course.	

A. Skevington Capt.
O.C.
99.- M.G.Cy.

99th Brigade / 2nd Division.

99th MACHINE GUN COMPANY ::: JULY 1917.

WAR DIARY
INTELLIGENCE SUMMARY

Army Form C. 2118

Place	Date	Hour	Summary of Events and Information	Remarks and references to Appendices
ANNEQUIN	July 1 to 20th Oct		Company in the line. 14 Guns in. In reserve at ANNEQUIN. Nothing further to report.	
	17th to 21st Oct			
	20th		2/Lt R.J GRIFFITH attends Lewis Course, 36th R.F.A.	
	20/21	10:30pm	Lt V. St. CLARE HILL returned from leave to U.K. 16 Guns of the Company assisted a Raiding party of the 23rd Royal Fusiliers by barrage fire. This proved most successful and prevented the enemy from approaching the raiding party. Rounds fired 5600. (S) Lt W Stretell attended Lewis Course 36th R.F.A	
	21/25			
	23.	9:15pm	14 Guns of this Company assisted by a barrage a raid of the 1st Leicestershire (71st Inf Bde) Rounds fired 41,000. Enemy retaliation was successfully drawn from the area to be raided.	
	24.		1 section (4 guns) was relieved by 1 section of our M.G Company the (Portons) taken over by them were R65, R64, V48, V45. One man bean[?] team[?] one officer and one cer[?] were left[?] for two inclusive purposes in this Coy.	Obtaining Capt Berendy 99 1955

WAR DIARY

INTELLIGENCE SUMMARY

Place	Date	Hour	Summary of Events and Information	Remarks and references to Appendices
ANNEQUIN	26		2/Lt WATSON and 2 ORs returned from course at GHQ Small Arms School, CAMIERS.	
		12.40 am	3 guns accurate rain by 2nd Lt 9. Rounds fired 7,500.	
	27		2/Lt R J Griffith and 4 ORs to A A Course 2/Lt A. PERRY and 2 ORs to Course at G2GR Small Arms School, CAMIERS.	
	28 29 30 31		Coy. in the lines. Nothing further to report.	

99th Brigade / 2nd Division.

99th MACHINE GUN COMPANY ::: AUGUST 1917.

Army Form C. 2118.

WAR DIARY
or
INTELLIGENCE SUMMARY

(Erase heading not required.)

99th M.G. Coy.

Vol 17

August 1917

Instructions regarding War Diaries and Intelligence Summaries are contained in F. S. Regs., Part II. and the Staff Manual respectively. Title Pages will be prepared in manuscript.

Place	Date	Hour	Summary of Events and Information	Remarks and references to Appendices

Army Form C. 2118.

WAR DIARY
or
INTELLIGENCE SUMMARY.
(Erase heading not required.)

Instructions regarding War Diaries and Intelligence Summaries are contained in F. S. Regs., Part II. and the Staff Manual respectively. Title pages will be prepared in manuscript.

Place	Date	Hour	Summary of Events and Information	Remarks and references to Appendices
ANNEQUIN	Aug 1.		Company in the line. 1 Guns in and 5 in reserve at ANNEQUIN	
	2/3/4.		2/Lt G E BACKHOUSE proceeded on Leave	
	5		Nothing to report	
			CAPT A.P. SKEVINGTON acting O.M.G.O	
			LIEUT V St CLARE HILL acting E.O.	
			4 teams of No 2 section relieved 1 team of No 3 section and	
			3 teams of No 4 section. No 4 section teams in turn relieved	
			3 teams of No 3 section. Whole of No 3 section to reserve	
			at Coy 3d.	
	6		2/Lt N ACKLAND took over R61 62 63 6d (portion)	
			2/Lt A.A. BUNDEY relieves LT. WALL	
	7/8/9		Nothing to report.	
	10		LT R.L WALL and LT C.W STRETTELL-MILLER admitted	
			to Hospital (sick). 2Lt N. ACKLAND a/T.O. vice 2 Lieut. J. LUNN.	
	11		Nothing to report.	
	12.		LT R.L WALL evacuated and struck off strength	
			2LT W. ACKLAND proceeds on Leave	
			2LT J. LUNN took over R61 62 63 64 (portions)	

Army Form C. 2118.

WAR DIARY
or
INTELLIGENCE SUMMARY.
(Erase heading not required.)

Instructions regarding War Diaries and Intelligence Summaries are contained in F. S. Regs., Part II. and the Staff Manual respectively. Title pages will be prepared in manuscript.

Place	Date	Hour	Summary of Events and Information	Remarks and references to Appendices
ANNEQUIN	13/14	10.30 pm and 2 am	6 guns of this Coy. and 3 guns of No 242 Coy Accroches by a barrage, raids by the Sherwood Foresters (139th Inf Bde). Rounds fired 43,000.	Attackowing by OC 99th Inf. Bgd.
	15		Lieut. J.A.WATSON relieved by 2LT G.E. BACKHOUSE.	
	16		Capt. A.P. SKEVINGTON resumes duties of Brigade M.G. Offr.	
	17		Capt. A.P. SKEVINGTON proceeds on leave. Lt V. ST CLARE HILL acting O.C.	
	18		Nothing to report.	
	19		2LT R.J. GRIFFITH from A.A. Course.	
	20		2LT R.J. GRIFFITH relieves 2LT M.A. BUNDEY.	
	21/24		Nothing to report.	
ANNEQUIN	25		2LT A.W. PERRY relieved 2LT J. LUNN 2LT J. LUNN proceeds on leave.	
ANNEQUIN			Part of Coy relieved by 139th M.G. Coy H.Qrs moves to ANNEZIN under LT. J.A. WATSON. Relief Commences 3 from LT V. ST CLARE HILL and 3 others and NCOs remainder to ANNEQUIN.	

Army Form C. 2118.

WAR DIARY
or
INTELLIGENCE SUMMARY
(Erase heading not required.)

Instructions regarding War Diaries and Intelligence Summaries are contained in F. S. Regs., Part II. and the Staff Manual respectively. Title Pages will be prepared in manuscript.

Place	Date	Hour	Summary of Events and Information	Remarks and references to Appendices
ANNE-ZIN.	26		LT V St CLARE HILL and remainder of Col. returned. 139th M.G Col. proceeded to ANNEZIN. Relief complete	Attached for 99th Brigade
	27		NIL.	
	28		Training in vicinity of billets	
	29		Training in vicinity of billets 2 O.R's proceeded to M.G School, CAMIERS "B" AA Battery for Course 2 O.R's "	
	30.		2/LT G.F. CLAUSEN reports for duty CAPT A.P. SKEVINGTON returned from Leave	
	31		CAPT A.P. SKEVINGTON proceeded to M.G School, CAMIERS for Course	

99th Brigade / 2nd Division.

99th MACHINE GUN COMPANY ::: SEPTEMBER 1917.

Army Form C. 2118.

WAR DIARY
INTELLIGENCE SUMMARY

(Erase heading not required.)

99th M.G. Coy.

Vol /8

September 1917.

Place	Date	Hour	Summary of Events and Information	Remarks and references to Appendices

Instructions regarding War Diaries and Intelligence Summaries are contained in F. S. Regs., Part II. and the Staff Manual respectively. Title Pages will be prepared in manuscript.

Army Form C. 2118.

WAR DIARY
INTELLIGENCE SUMMARY
(Erase heading not required.)

Place	Date	Hour	Summary of Events and Information	Remarks and references to Appendices
ANNEZIN	1/9/17		Company parades in vicinity of billets.	Lt Col G. F. Coll
	2/3/4/5th		Company prepared to resume into Givenchy - Festubert Sector.	
ANNEZIN GORRE	6th		The company relieved 6th M.G. Coy in the line in Givenchy - Festubert Sector. 2nd Lt Lewis returned from leave.	
"	7th		Relief complete by 2AM. No 3 section proceeded to the line under 2nd Lt Craven.	
LE PLANTIN	8-14th		Company in line. Harrassing fire eased night against enemy working parties.	
	15th		Lt Wall rejoined from M.G.C. Base Depôt.	
	16.		Company in line. Nothing to report.	
	17		Company relieved in the line by the 6th M.G. Coy. On relief proceeded to billets in Beuvry. 2nd Lt Perry proceeded on leave.	
	18.		Relief complete by 2AM. Company rested in Beuvry.	
ANNEQUIN	19th		Company relieved 135th M.G. Coy in Cambrin Sector. Coy H.Q. at Annequin Fosse.	
	20th 21st 22 23 24		Company in line. 1 Section afternoon relieved by 242nd M.G.Coy. Company in the line.	

2449 Wt. W14957/M90 750,000 1/16 J.B.C. & A. Forms/C.2118/12.

Army Form C. 2118.

WAR DIARY
INTELLIGENCE SUMMARY
(Erase heading not required.)

Instructions regarding War Diaries and Intelligence Summaries are contained in F. S. Regs., Part II and the Staff Manual respectively. Title Pages will be prepared in manuscript.

Place	Date	Hour	Summary of Events and Information	Remarks and references to Appendices
ANNEQUIN	25.		Company in the line. ANNEQUIN FOSSE shelled with 8" Howitzers & gas were discharged by the enemy through the mist	
	26.		ANNEQUIN FOSSE again shelled. Coy H.Q. moved to ANNEQUIN NORTH Intercommunication relief.	
	27.		Capt. A. P. STEVINGTON returned from leave at CANIERS.	
	28.		Quiet day	
	29.		do	
	30.		2nd Lt. PERRY returned from leave	
			(Harassing every night & stilled the company were in the line in conjunction with Artillery support.)	

99th Brigade / 2nd Division.

99th MACHINE GUN COMPANY ::: OCTOBER 1917.

WAR DIARY
INTELLIGENCE SUMMARY
(Erase heading not required)

Army Form C. 2118.

99th Machine Gun Coy

Vol 19

For October 1917.

Instructions regarding War Diaries and Intelligence Summaries are contained in F. S. Regs., Part II. and the Staff Manual respectively. Title pages will be prepared in manuscript.

Place	Date	Hour	Summary of Events and Information	Remarks and references to Appendices

Army Form C. 2118.

WAR DIARY
INTELLIGENCE SUMMARY
(Erase heading not required.)

Instructions regarding War Diaries and Intelligence Summaries are contained in F. S. Regs., Part II. and the Staff Manual respectively. Title pages will be prepared in manuscript.

Place	Date	Hour	Summary of Events and Information	Remarks and references to Appendices
ANNEQUIN NORTH CAMBRIN SECTOR	1917 Oct. 1		Company in the line. Harassing fire was carried out between 8pm & 10pm on selected targets in conjunction with 1/5" & 4.6" Batteries R.F.A. Firing continued at intervals during the night.	
	" 2		ditto	
	" 3		ditto	
	" 4	11.30pm	Coy was relieved by Special Coy. R.E. M.G. Barrage & artillery cooperation. Officers & N.C.O's of 74th M.G. Coy reconnoitred the line before taking over.	
ANNEZIN & OBLINGHEM	" 5		Coy relieved on the line by 74th M.G. Coy. On relief the Coy moved to new billets in OBLINGHEM. Coy arrived at 6.30pm	
AUCHEL	" 6		Coy marched to AUCHEL via ANNEZIN - LABEUVRIERE - LAPUGNOY - MARIES LES MINES - AUCHEL. Coy proceeded at 6.30am & arrived at AUCHEL at 1.10pm	
	" 7		Quiet day (Sunday)	
	" 8-13"		Coy inoculated in vicinity of billets. On the 13" O.C. to 11th (Army) Infantry School. Lau F. G. CIPRE-HIES a/o.c.	
	" 14"		Brigade Church parade or 1/KRR C/parade opened at 10.30 AM. Addresses by the Bishop of KHARTOUM	
	" 15"		Capt Moon proceeded to A. A. Course GASNAY. 99" Inf Bde inspected by Army Commander for Army. Coy paraded at 10.15 AM. Inspection at 11.30 AM	

Wilkinson Capt.

(A7092) Wt. W12839/M1293. 75,000. 4/17. D. D. & L., Ltd. Forms/C2118/14.

Army Form C. 2118.

WAR DIARY

or

~~INTELLIGENCE SUMMARY~~

(Erase heading not required.)

Instructions regarding War Diaries and Intelligence Summaries are contained in F. S. Regs., Part II. and the Staff Manual respectively. Title pages will be prepared in manuscript.

Place	Date	Hour	Summary of Events and Information	Remarks and references to Appendices
AUCHEL	1917 Oct 16		Coy parades in vicinity of billets. L/Sgt Stewart & Pte Stephens to 1st Army Rest Camp. 2nd Lt L Stopford Waldman & Sumpett to Brigade Bombing Course. O.C. returned from XVIIIth Corps School. L/Sgt Woodman & Sumpett to Brigade Bombing Course. Senior N.C.O.s at AUCHEL in evening. Inter section football in afternoon.	
	17		Lecture on Artillery Work by Major	
	18	6.15pm	Coy parades in vicinity of billets.	
CAUCHY-A-LA-TOUR	19		Baths. Coy moved to CAUCHY-A-LA-TOUR.	
	20		Coy parades in vicinity of billets. Coy passed through Gas Chamber.	
	21		Nos 1 & 2 Sections on the range at FERFAY.	
	22		Coy Church Parade. Lts V. St. CLARE-HILL & J.A. WATSON proceeded on leave to U.K. L/Sgts Tune & Cpl Moore returned from A.A. Course GOSNAY. Lt R.L. WALL attended O.C. proceeded to ST JANS-TER-BIEZEN for conference with O.C. M.G. Coys. Lt F.J.R. GRIFFITH returned from leave. Command of the Coy. Coy parades in vicinity of billets.	
	23		Coy parades for tactical scheme	
	24		Parades in vicinity of billets	
	25		Brigade Tactical Scheme. O.O. attacked. Coy parades not marched off at 7.30 a.m. Returned 2 p.m.	
	26		Coy parades in vicinity of billets. O.C. returned from 9 days leave. command.	
	27		Nos 3 & 4 Sections on range in afternoon at FERFAY.	
	28		C.O's inspection. Church Parade. 2nd Lt LUNN admitted to hospital.	
	29		Coy parades in vicinity of billets. Bath. T.T. Robinson attached for 3 days. L/Cpl Raine proceeded to LA BEUVRIÈRE on 4 days Gas Course. Lantern Lecture on aircraft photographs at AUCHEL CINEMA.	
	30		Route March training in vicinity of billets. 10. O. attached.	
	31		Coy moved off at 7.45 A.M. preliminary at 1 p.m.	

Tactical Scheme

(A7094) Wt. W12859/M1293 75,000. 1/17. D. D. & L., Ltd. Forms/C.2118/14.

Secret.   Copy No. 1

99th Machine Gun Coy
Operation Order No 80.   C.26.b.80.05
                                                          25-10-17

Reference Maps Sheet 36B N.W. 1/20,000.
        and attached tracing

1. The 99th Infantry Brigade have received orders to attack, capture and consolidate the enemy positions on the ridge in C.10 and C.16. Other troops are co-operating on the flanks. Enemy occupy MARLES LES MINES, LOZINGHEM and ALLOUAGNE, also the high ground in Square C.10 and C.16.

2. a. Two guns of No 1 Section under the command of 2/Lt A.H. BUNDEY will go forward about Z +30 on the RIGHT FLANK of RIGHT SECTOR to assist the 23rd Royal Fusiliers in consolidation of first objective.

   Two guns of No 1 Section under the command of 2/Lt R.J. GRIFFITH will go forward about Z +30 on the LEFT FLANK of LEFT SECTOR to assist the 1st Royal Berks in consolidation of first objective.

   When the second objective has been gained and is in course of being consolidated the officers in charge of the above 4 guns will reconnoitre up to the second objective with a view to assisting in the defence thereof and will place their guns accordingly, reporting their action to the officers commanding areas concerned.

b. The four guns of No 4 Section under the Command of 2/Lt. G.E. BACKHOUSE will standby in Reserve at C.8.b.90.00.

c. The guns of Nos 2 and 3 Sections will form a battery for overhead barrage fire on 1st and 2nd objectives in accordance with Artillery programme. Battery position C.8.d. Central.

One Section of 242nd. M.G. Coy (imaginary) will take up battery position at C.2.d.60.20 to assist in overhead barrage fire on 1st and 2nd objectives.

One Section of 242nd M.G. Coy (imaginary) will take up battery position at C.2.d.70.30 for overhead fire on wood at C.10.d.30.20.

All M.G. Batteries will fire in Conjunction with Artillery Time Table.

3. Communications.

Officers Commdg. M.G. Sections will make arrangements for Communication with O.C., 99th M.G. Coy. at Bde H.Q. at C.9.a.30.00.

M.G. Batteries will be in inter Communication by telephone.

- 3 -

Dumps.

S.A.A.
A dump of 200,000 rounds will be situated close to road at C8a.70.40. for the use of Batteries at C8d Central and at C2d.70.30 to be ready there by 4 p.m. on "Y" day. The exact position of this dump will be selected by the Battery Commanders.

A dump of 50,000 rounds will be situated in valley about C9b.40.00.

Rations and Water.

2 Petrol Tins of water per gun team and rations will be at same positions as S.A.A. dumps.

5. **Medical Arrangements.**

Casualties from teams going forward and Reserve Guns will report to Battn. Aid Post.

6. **Synchronisation of Watches.**

A watch with which Section watches will be synchronised will be sent round by runner at 5 a.m.

7. ZERO HOUR 10 A.M.

8. Transport Arrangements

a. The 4 fighting limbers of Nos 2 & 3 Sections will carry guns and gun equipment to respective battery positions during "Y" night; after unloading will stand by at Cross Roads C.80.20.20 and await further orders.

b. 12 pack animals will carry guns and ammunition for forward positions as far forward as possible on "Y" night.

Thence carriage will be by Yukon packs and Tumpline.

9. ACKNOWLEDGE.

Lieut
Commdg. A.W. Machine Gun Coy

Issued to:

1, 2. War Diary.
3. Office Copy.
4, 5, 6. O & C Sections
7.
8, 9, 10, 11. Battn Commds.
12. Brigade H.Q.
13. D.A.D.O.
14. Tr Battn.
15. Transport Officer.

SECRET.   R.L.W.   COPY No.

99th Machine Gun Company.   C.26.b.50.05.

Operation Order No. 81   31.10.17

Ref. Map.
    Sheet 36^B N.W. 1/20,000.
    and attached Sketch Map.

1. The British hold LOZINGHEM, AUCHEL, and
Camps à la Tour with their advanced troops
on an approximate N.E. and S.W. line
through the Eastern edge of the wood in
C.17.c. and the level crossing at C.15.d.2.0
facing N.W.

    The 99th Infantry Brigade will attack,
capture and consolidate the high ground
in Squares C.9. and 10. Other Divisions
are co-operating on either flank.

    The Germans hold BURBURE and the
high ground to the East C.9. and 10. with
advanced posts and strong points on a
line C.10.d.9.0., LAMBERT WOOD, RAILWAY
FOSSE, facing South.

– 2 –

No 1. Section, under 2nd Lt A.A.BURREY, will form up, in and close to the British front line immediately behind the 22nd ROYAL FUSILIERS, on the Left Sector. They will advance immediately behind the Infantry and take up a position under cover in or about RUMBERT WOOD.
On the First Objective being taken, they will go forward and take up positions approximately at :-

No 2. Section, under 2nd Lt R.J.GRIFFITH, will form up, in and close to the British front line immediately behind the 1st K.R.R.C. on the Right Sector. They will advance immediately behind the Infantry and take up a position about 200 yards in advance of British front line.
On the First Objective being taken, they will go forward and take up positions approximately at :-

No 3. Section, under 2nd Lt A.H.PERRY, will form up immediately behind the 23rd ROYAL FUSILIERS, on the Left Sector and will advance with them and take up a position about 200 yards in front of the British front line. On the British line going forward they will go forward to the following approximate positions :-

For Consolidation.
No 4. Section, under 2nd Lt G.E.BACKHOUSE, will form up immediately behind the 1st ROYAL BERKSHIRE Regt, on the Right Sector and will advance with them and take under cover in or about

— 3 —

in C.10.d.
the wood. On the second objective being taken, they will go forward to following approximate position:—

for consolidation.

The approximate fields of fire for the 16 Guns when situated in the availed [positions].

Barrage fires under command of the D.M.G.O. are imaginary.

Communication.
Officer Commanding M.G. Section will make Arrangements for communication by runner to O.C. 69th M.G. Company at Brigade Headquarters at Y of CEMETERY (C.22.a.7.3.) and also keep in close touch with the O.C. Section in case further means is needed for urgent communications. Further details see M.G. Appendix A, to be issued later.

4. Dumps
Full details re. Dumps, S.A.A., Rations, water and loads will be issued later in M.G. Appendix B.

5. Medical Arrangements — to be issued later
6. Synchronisation of watches.
The watches will be synchronised will be sent round at 5 a.m.

7. ZERO HOUR
10. A.M.

— 4 —

8. **Transport Arrangements**
   Transport will be under the orders of 2nd Lt. W. ACKLAND.

9. **Artillery Programme** — attached

10. **ACKNOWLEDGE**

                                    Captain
                            Commanding 99th Machine Gun Coy

Issued to :-
1.)   8.)
2.) War Diary.   9.) Battalion Commanders.
3.) Office Copy   10.)
4.)   11.)
5.) O.C. Sections.   12. Brigade.
6.)   13. D.M.G.O.
7.)   14. T.M. Battery
                             15. Transport Officer.

99th Brigade / 2nd Division.

99th MACHINE GUNCOMPANY :::: NOVEMBER 1917.

WAR DIARY
or
INTELLIGENCE SUMMARY.

94th Machine Gun Coy.
November 1917.

Vol 20

Army Form C. 2118

WAR DIARY
of
INTELLIGENCE SUMMARY

99th Machine Gun Coy.

(Erase heading not required)

Instructions regarding War Diaries and Intelligence Summaries are contained in F.S. Regs., Part II. and the Staff Manual respectively. Title pages will be prepared in manuscript.

Place	Date	Hour	Summary of Events and Information	Remarks and references to Appendices
CAUCHY à la TOUR.	1/11/17		Coy remained in billets at CAUCHY-à-la-TOUR. Tactical Exercises and training carried out in vicinity of billets.	
	2/11/17		1st Lieut. V.G. Blane, Lieut. Leavemore and 2nd Sgt. J.S. Watson returned from Leave. Coy proceeded to XVIII Corps School VOLKERINGHOVE for course.	
	3/11/17		Coy paraded about 8.30am and marched to ROBECK.	
ROBECK	5/11/17		Coy marched from ROBECK to ESTAIRÉS. Capt. ROBERTS proceeds to M.G. School CAMIERS for course.	
ESTAIRÉS	6/11/17		Coy marched from ESTAIRÉS to EECKE.	
EECKE	7/11/17		Coy marched from EECKE to WINNEZEELE.	
WINNEZEELE	8/11/17		Lieut. R.L. HALL proceeded on leave to U.K.	
"	9/11/17 – 22/11/17		Coy carried out training in vicinity of billets, including Coy Tactical Schemes and Ly grades. 19th 11/17 & 21st 11/17 Coy moved to prepare to move at very short notice to Blank. Orders here received during the period to bring the Coy in all respects up to War Establishment.	
"	22/11/17		Coy received orders to be ready to move at 2 hours notice. Coy sports keen the afternoon.	

(A7092) Wt. W12859/M1293. 75,000. 1/17. D.D. & L., Ltd. Forms/C2118/14.

Army Form C. 2118

WAR DIARY
INTELLIGENCE SUMMARY
(Erase heading not required)

99th Inf. Coy.

Place	Date	Hour	Summary of Events	Remarks and references to Appendices

WINNEZEELE 23/11/17

Reveille 5am
The transport proceeded by road to ESQUELBECK
– via HERZEELE and WORMHOUDT – and entrained

8.30am Coy. (less transport) paraded, marched to ESQUELBECK and entrained at 10pm

Coy. arrived at ACHIET-LE-GRAND at 4.5am 24th Nov. and detrained

Coy. marched to "D" Camp BARASTRE arriving at 4.5am

BARASTRE 24/11/17
Coy. rested, under canvas, at "D" Camp BARASTRE

BEAUMETZ 25/11/17 LES-CAMBRAI
8.30am Coy. paraded and marched to BEAUMETZ-LES-CAMBRAI. Billets under canvas.

" 26/11/17
Coy. rested. Orders received for Coy. to prepare to take over the line in the Sector 31st Coy. BACKHOUSE proceeded to the line from leave

Capt
R.S. Backhouse
16.99th M.G. Coy.

WAR DIARY
INTELLIGENCE SUMMARY

99th M.G. Coy

Place	Date	Hour	Summary of Events
BEAUMETZ LES-CAMBRAI	27/11/17		Capt. A.P. Skevington. O.C. proceeds to the line for information prior to taking over. 11 pm. Nebot Sec, 7 new by Sec. trausport and H.Q. details proceed to the line and took over positions in the Sector Transport Lines and Rear HQ established near HERMIES. 9th A. SLAG HEAP near the line. 4 Sec Section taken into the line, H Sec Section. 16 Guns arrived. Capt A.P. Skevington. O.C., Officers at Aid post. 7 Pl. Plane still in Command. Sent officers to sections No 1 L¹. R. L. Wall No 2 L⁰. R. Lynch and Alsbury No 3 L¹. Jackson No 4 2¹⁶. G.C. Backhouse and A. Wilson

WAR DIARY / INTELLIGENCE SUMMARY

Army Form C. 2118.

99th M.G. Coy

Place	Date	Hour	Summary of Events and Information	Remarks and references to Appendices
Tooper the Line	28/11/17		1 O.R wounded slightly	
	29/11/17		Coy in the line. 6C made a general reconnaissance of the positions occupied by the Company. Quiet activity of enemy. Heavy walking, registering on the trenches and firing pinpoint towards the evening. His enemy laid down a barrage for barrage the evening being 50 yards short. 4 O.Rs wounded. His registration	ReLelly Lt
	30/11/17	About 9:30 Am	the enemy laid down and intensive barrage in accordance with his practice of the evening before. Reports were received to the effect that the enemy were massing in large numbers on our left flank and on the sunken track in the rear. All guns were immediately informed and ordered to be in readiness. Almost immediately a report was received that the enemy were massing on our right and that the light artillery could be seen coming up behind by advancing infantry. This looks and still in view to bring tip an attack. The right were moved in order to bring fire on two guns in being our breakout front. At 10.30 am the enemy our left than advancing in to leave. two guns in a launched his attack and advancing in front of the infantry situated forward of outline 8 Hills 0 Yards from 6 Belstrew & the infantry of the enemy in a were garrisoned	

WAR DIARY or INTELLIGENCE SUMMARY

Army Form C. 2118

Place	Date	Hour	Summary of Events and Information	Remarks and references to Appendices
	30/10/17		O'mies fire at a range of 1800 yards by Lewis Guns immediately opened fire on the right flank enemy to charge his flanks and to press to my right flank the enemy soon extended front that two guns and buffered [?] in the thus left and [?] he was approaching the back from the left. Also the two [?] ins[?] in the high field [?] moved to my right [?] casualties forced gun [?] in the enemy but he came in such numbers [?] on this approach and the enemy [?] with them. The officer of [?] men upon the gun could not [?] church and [?] ordered the withdrawal that the second line [?] he was about [?] yards where withdrawn myseparated to [?] sunken road along the garden were also withdrawn as the enemy [?] the [?] post of the [?] place and as the enemy Yes. The 2 guns could not formed a [?] here on [?] attention [?] CHURCH TRENCH and formed a withdrawal firing to the casualties to personnel were hearing hard stay along the casualties to personnel [?] [?] the withdrawal owing to the casualties to personnel [?] guns were abandoned. The two guns were advancing rapidly on our front and [?] to it was advancing rapidly on our front and 8 guns meanwhile in the direction of BOISLON WOOD. The casualties two [?] proceeding in the 200 yards right of the CANAL CUT was [?] in our front in influencing is such fire is situated in our influence with higher [?] over advancing to higher [?] [?] advancing to [?] enemy in [?] guns were wounded which was obviously dead [?] on a force of guns inflicted such casualties [?] Enemy two division again that the enemy were [?]

Army Form C. 2118.

WAR DIARY
or
INTELLIGENCE SUMMARY.
(Erase heading not required.)

Place	Date	Hour	Summary of Events and Information	Remarks and references to Appendices
	30/1/17.		The Division took the Centre and the right of the Brigade frontage & a rise to our right. Enemy Gun numbering Regt were quickly came under our own and enemy Rifle were put out of enfilade m.g. fire and the attack was completely dismounted. 3.O.R.s killed. 1 Off. wounded (slight) It was Cnfsdty... Casualties were. about 8.30 p.m. 2 guns were about 250 yards 12 O.R.s wounded. 9 O.R.s missing 3 damaged his able to the Enemy Completely obstinged by shellfire . in Emergency.	A.R.Thomson Lt Col.

99th Brigade / 2nd Division.

99th MACHINE GUN COMPANY ::: DECEMBER 1917.

Army Form C. 2118.

WAR DIARY
or
INTELLIGENCE SUMMARY.
(Erase heading not required.)

99th M.G. Coy.

Vol 21

December 1917

Place	Date	Hour	Summary of Events and Information	Remarks and references to Appendices

WAR DIARY
INTELLIGENCE SUMMARY

Army Form C. 2118.

Place	Date	Hour	Summary of Events and Information	Remarks and references to Appendices
Ref Map E.27	1-4 Dec		Refugee Sheet. MOEUVRES 20.000	
			Guns in the line. HQrs at E.26.b.40.30	
K.20b	Nov 4/5		Guns and conf HQrs withdrawn to K.20b (Spoilheap, Hermies) Transport Lines and Leg HQrs moved from SLAG HEAP Phu	
	6		to VELU WOOD.	
	11		New Battery positions taken up at K.11 and K.15 (Refuser Transport and Jant 60.95 (6 guns) HQrs in Huron at Transport Lines.	Willoughby Kerr Lt Penning 99 Sqdn
	17		2Lt T.L TIMPERLEY joined Col.	
			2Lt A.H BUNDEY to leave to UK	
	24		2Lt W ACKLAND to leave to UK	
	26		Lt V.S. Blackshaw to Course "Use of m/gs" A.G.'s General Con Flying Aircraft" 68th Squadron RFC BAZIEUX	

WAR DIARY
INTELLIGENCE SUMMARY.
(Erase heading not required.)

Army Form C. 2118.

Place	Date	Hour	Summary of Events and Information	Remarks and references to Appendices
K30b	27		Captain A.P. Kerington to Major Oppen 186. at 1200. Officer (M.G.) and Ja. Watson assumed command of Coy.	
	28		Battery position at K.11.d. 40b6 relieved by 64 M. Bty. Guns taken up A.a. portion for Antiaircraft Defence at K36a 70.10. K25a 18, K27a Central, T24b 8160	
	31		Lt. I.L. TIMPERLEY to course at M.G. Training Centre Grantham	

www.ingramcontent.com/pod-product-compliance
Lightning Source LLC
Chambersburg PA
CBHW081426200426
R18167200001B/R181672PG43193CBX00001B/1